TALES FROM THE
DODGER
DUGOUT

TOMMY DAVIS
WITH PAUL GUTIERREZ

www.SportsPublishingLLC.com

ISBN: 1-58261-756-2

Publishers: Peter L. Bannon and Joseph J. Bannon Sr.
Senior managing editor: Susan M. Moyer
Acquisitions editor: Mike Pearson
Developmental editor: Doug Hoepker
Art director: K. Jeffrey Higgerson
Book design: Jennifer L. Polson
Dust jacket design: Kenneth J. O'Brien
Imaging: Heidi Norsen
Photo editor: Erin Linden-Levy
Vice president of sales and marketing: Kevin King
Media and promotions managers: Jonathan Patterson (regional), Randy Fouts (national), Maurey Williamson (print)

Printed in the United States

Sports Publishing L.L.C.
804 North Neil Street
Champaign, IL 61820

Phone: 1-877-424-2665
Fax: 217-363-2073
Web site: www.SportsPublishingLLC.com

I'd like to thank my parents, Grace and Herman Sr.,
who gave me life, taught me values and to never give up
and to respect people.

To my wife, Carol, and all of my family for supporting me
through the thick and thin, the highs and the lows.

And to my children—Lauren, Michelle, Leslie Grace,
Carlyn Thomasa, Herman Thomas III, and Morgana Tie—
whom I love dearly.

A special thanks to Mr. Clarence Irving, who taught me
the value of team play in the game of baseball, and to all the
people from the beginning in Brooklyn and all the way to the people
at the end in California. To all of my teammates, from the
Brooklyn Bisons to 10 major league teams, especially the Dodgers,
thank you. It was truly a blessing to be associated with guys like
Sandy Koufax, Jim Gilliam, Maury Wills, Johnny Roseboro
and my roomie Willie Davis.

T.D.

To my muse, my number-one "producer," my wife, Amy.
Thank you for your patience, understanding and wisdom.
And to my newborn son, Zach, can't wait to share some tales
with you, mijo. And to my parents, Lorraine and Henry, and my
brother James, thanks for believing.

P.G.

CONTENTS

FOREWORD
BY MAURY WILLS

WHEN TOMMY ASKED ME to write the foreword for his book, I have to admit that I was taken aback a bit. I've always known that Tommy thought well of me as an individual and as a teammate, but I was really flattered. There's a whole bunch of guys from our teams that he could have asked, so I wonder how many turned him down before he got to me?

But seriously, it's an honor. Anybody else, I probably would have said no, turned them down flat. But Tommy saw me at my pinnacle and also at rock bottom, when I was strung out and surrendering to a power greater than myself. I knew it all back then, I knew every damn thing. But the truth is, I didn't know anything. Tommy saw me when I was in my demise, and to come all the way back and be asked by Tommy to write the foreword to his book, it's a blessing beyond my wildest dreams.

Tommy likes to say that we've had a love-hate relationship throughout the years, but that might be a bit too strong. Tommy has a sense of humor that's a little sickening and it rubbed me the wrong way. It would fire me up to a point. Now, though, with my new approach to life, I just say, "Tommy, I'll keep praying for you." He just keeps that shit-ass grin on his face. It must have come from Brooklyn.

What was funny was how close we were off the field. One summer, I rented Willie Davis's house in Baldwin Hills and I lived four doors down from Tommy, and in the mornings my kids would go over and play with Tommy's kids and we'd have coffee together. Then we'd get to the park and be in each other's faces all game long.

I guess our run-ins reached a crescendo when we were in Milwaukee and I bought a nice Dodger Blue sweater with a crew-neck collar and long sleeves. It was 70 degrees so it was a little warm for a sweater, but I liked it. I could see the wheels turning and Tommy started in on me right away. Well, you can read all about that incident in Chapter 4.

I challenged him to fight a couple of times, even though he outweighed me by about a hundred pounds. Love-hate? We were more like Tom and Jerry, the cat and mouse cartoons, the way we went after each other. Guess who was the mouse? We loved each other like brothers. We won pennants and World Series with that kind of fire.

The media was different then, they didn't report certain things. About 10 to 12 years after we finished playing, when I was locked up in my house battling my alcohol and drug problems, Tommy and his wife, Carol, often came over to visit with me. He didn't come down on me. He didn't preach to me. He just came over and kept me company. I'll never forget that. That's why he's a good person to tell the tales of the Dodgers' Golden Age in Los Angeles—he's a good person who was always in the middle. I can't think of one person whom Tommy showed a dislike toward—maybe the manager—but I was the only one he had a spat with, and it was essentially just having fun.

That's Tommy to a T. He's kind of a mischievous guy. He's not of the same serious nature as I am, or Sandy Koufax or Don Drysdale or Johnny Roseboro, to name a few. Tommy's a happy-go-lucky guy, and after reading this book, I'm sure you'll feel the same.

ACKNOWLEDGMENTS

THE AUTHORS WOULD LIKE TO ACKNOWLEDGE the assistance of many without whom this project would not have gotten off the ground, let alone been possible. Those who need to be commended for taking the time to share their tales: Maury Wills, Lou Johnson, Tommy Lasorda, Vin Scully, Stu Nahan, Ron Fairly, Bill "Moose" Skowron, Sandy Koufax, Nate Oliver and Wes Parker. Also, Chris Gutierrez of John Olguin's media relations staff with the Dodgers, for his help in securing numerous photos and the team's own reflections of the 1963 World Series; and team historian Mark Langill, also for help in hunting and gathering pictures and for answering numerous fact-checking calls and e-mails; and the Dodger organization itself. And, of course, the good folks at Sports Publishing, including Mike Pearson, whose vision was the genesis for this book, and Doug Hoepker, whose editing allowed these tales to see the light of day. Again, thanks to all.

T.D. and P.G.

INTRODUCTION
BY PAUL GUTIERREZ

IT WAS LATE on one of those muggy summer afternoons in Los Angeles, a typical Southern California day when you can cut through the "hazy sunshine" with a knife. The crack of the bat meeting the ball echoed throughout the empty baseball shrine, still just as glorious and gleaming as it was 42 years ago. We were at Dodger Stadium, the Dodgers were taking batting practice, hours before the first pitch of their game that night, and I was doing my best to be a fly on the wall.

It's called Blue Heaven on Earth and really, is there a better place to help get the memory juices flowing for players who ruled this roost four decades ago? I was meeting with Tommy Davis, and he had invited Maury Wills to join us to share his thoughts on the Golden Age of the Dodgers in Los Angeles. Though we were sitting in the orange seats, the exclusive loge level behind home plate, a campfire with roasted marshmallows and Dodgerdogs would not have been out of place for this story time. As I listened in, furiously scribbling in my notebook, the years melted off of Tommy and Maury.

Suddenly, it was 1962 again, the year the stadium opened. You could feel the reverberations of long-departed fans chanting, "Go, Go, Go," to Maury, imploring him to steal a base. You could sense a ghostly crowd's anticipation whenever Tommy came to the plate that year, a season in which he became the first and still only Los Angeles Dodger to lead the National League in batting average and runs batted in. Inevitably, a sense of sorrow and pent-up anger followed, the duo reliving that season's epic collapse at the hands of the hated San Francisco Giants. I had grown up with the Dodgers of Garvey, Cey, Lopes and Russell, came of age during the height of Fernandomania and was a recent high school graduate when Kirk Gibson hit his dramatic home run into the right-field pavilion in Game 1 of the 1988 World Series. The Dodgers had won two World

Series titles in seven years of my youth and I thought my generation was spoiled. That is, until I told my dad about the project I was about to undertake.

"Tommy Davis? Really?" my dad asked. "He was my hero." Those Dodgers were heroes to an entire generation who still look back fondly on those first years in Los Angeles as a more innocent and successful time. The Dodgers, who moved to L.A. in 1958, had won one World Series in 68 years in Brooklyn. One. In the club's first nine years in the Southland, they went to four World Series and won three of them. Names such as Davis, Wills, Koufax and Drysdale were baseball royalty in the days of JFK's Camelot, which made my job of helping Tommy chronicle and re-tell the history of the team from that era all the more challenging and intriguing.

For those that were there—players and fans—it would be a chance to revel in the past. And for those who weren't, it's an opportunity to learn about and pay respect to an era that is still felt around Dodger Stadium today.

Hence, my desire to become that omnipresent fly on the wall. I had my own time machine as Tommy and Maury suddenly became that old married couple that I had read and heard so much about. They were the epitome of the love-hate relationship. Especially when Tommy kept trying to correct Maury on the facts of when they first met—in a spring training sprint race on a Vero Beach field.

"C'mon, Tommy, get out of my shit," Maury said. "You want me to tell the story or what?"

He tells it, as do many other former Dodgers. That the stories are like wine, getting better with age, is but a bonus. By the time you turn the last page of the book, I hope you've had as much educational fun reading it as I did in helping Tommy write it.

Paul Gutierrez
South Pasadena, California
November, 2004

1

GROWING UP A
DODGERS FAN
IN BROOKLYN

A Natural Fit

I'm from Brooklyn. I grew up in Bedford-Stuyvesant and was a Brooklyn Dodgers fan, naturally, because of Jackie Robinson coming into the National League in 1947. Jackie created a lot of excitement. He wasn't a small man. He was about six-foot-one, 200 pounds, but he ran the bases like he was a track star. He stole a lot of bases, swiping home several times, and just created a lot of excitement for the people of Brooklyn.

A lot of Dodger home games were on TV back then. From 1947 until 1956 they went to six World Series, all against one damn team—the New York Yankees. That's unbelievable. And in my family, we were all Brooklyn Dodgers fans except for my mother's brother, Dan Smith. He was a Yankees fan and a big guy—about 6-2, 300 pounds with a voice just as loud. He'd stop by and ridicule us all the time, "We beat your butts again." We just closed the door and he enjoyed it immensely. But the year that we won our first World Series, in 1955, he left town. We sent him telegrams, all kinds of stuff. But even if he never liked the Dodgers, he became a Tommy Davis fan when I made the majors.

Opportunity Missed

Naturally I would have loved to have played in Brooklyn. I don't know if that would have been good or bad with my friends around. I might have spent too much time hanging out. But playing in Los Angeles worked out because I wouldn't have met my wife of today if I hadn't left Brooklyn for Los Angeles. Being away from home, I could pay a little more attention to the game itself, which I did.

You know, the people in Brooklyn still believe the Dodgers are coming back some day. They are still hurt by the Dodgers leaving town. I know I hurt. I was hurting because I was still in the minor leagues when they left. So after that it became more of a business. I just had to make it then.

I was very disappointed because Brooklyn is a special place. It's just a borough but it's known all over the world. The Dodgers didn't have "New York" in front of their name. They had the New York Giants and the New York Yankees and now the New York Mets. But there's only one Brooklyn Dodgers.

Finding a Niche

The Cleveland Indians were the first to scout me. Merv Frankel was a friend of mine and he was a bird dog for Cleveland. He was the first person to talk to me when I was a junior in high school. At the time I was long-jumping for Boys High School in the city final under a different name—Tommy Washington—because I was playing baseball under my real name. I also played basketball for Boys

Ebbets Field was more than a bandbox for "Dem Bums" and their fans, who were unbelievably close to the action; it was a second home for any baseball-loving kid who grew up in Brooklyn. Courtesy of the Los Angeles Dodgers

High and was an all-city player along with Lenny Wilkens. Connie Hawkins came later and played at my high school, too.

Right next door to the track meet was Yankee Stadium and I had a tryout with Cleveland there and I qualified for the finals in the long jump. But I left before the finals and went and worked out with Cleveland. I was in right field with Rocky Colavito. My high school guys called me up later and said, "We lost by five points. We lost the title by just five points." I said, "Ah, that's terrible." They didn't want to hear it. They said, "You could have made the difference." So I thought for a minute, "Oh that's right, I did qualify for the final."

So they said, "I suggest you better not come to school for a while." So, I didn't go to school for a while.

Later on, I went to Philadelphia and worked out for the Phillies too. I was trying to make it as a catcher, but every time I worked out, the same thing would happen. I'd get moved to second base, or the outfield. I would run a race and beat everybody. That's when they told me, "You ain't no catcher. Get out to the outfield."

Because of Jackie

I was scouted by the Dodgers' Al Campanis, but the Yankees gave me more attention, to the point where I had a locker at Yankee Stadium. Any time I wanted to work out, I just called them. I did that for a while. But Al Campanis kept coming around, keeping his two cents in there. I guess he found out I was going to sign with the Yankees on a Tuesday afternoon and he had Jackie Robinson call me on Sunday night. That did it. All I needed to hear was Jackie's voice. That's all it took. That Tuesday afternoon I signed with the Dodgers. Jackie didn't have to say anything to me—just the sound of his voice sold me. But he told me that the Dodgers would look after me and that they had good instructors. And they also had quite a few black ballplayers, Campy and Newcombe and Dan Bankhead and Joe Black and Jim Gilliam. That made a big impression on me. But if Jackie Robinson would have been the only black on the team, I think I still would have signed with the Dodgers.

When he called, he said, "This is Jackie Robinson. I'd like to talk to you about the advantages of signing with the Dodgers, what to look forward to. They treat me good and under the circumstances, they're going to look out for you." To tell you the truth, I don't remember what he said after that. After I heard, "This is Jackie Robinson," I just about dropped the phone.

I wanted to sign with the Dodgers in the first place—because of Jackie—but they just didn't show me that much attention. I was also a pretty good basketball player in high school, too. Lenny

Jackie Robinson was a hero to many, myself included. He was so proud that when the Dodgers showed him the door by doing the unthinkable and trading him to the hated Giants, he simply retired rather than wear their colors. Courtesy of the Los Angeles Dodgers

Wilkens wanted me to go with him to Providence. Ohio State wanted me to go there for baseball and the Kiwanis Club wanted to give me a scholarship to go to Northwestern. But I would have had to go to a prep school first, and I just wanted to play ball. With the Dodgers.

Bittersweet Beginning

When I signed with the Dodgers in 1956, it was Jackie's last year. The Dodgers actually traded him to the Giants. That was a slap in the face, boy. But he retired rather than become a Giant. Sure, I was sad that I wasn't able to play with Jackie. He was my hero. When I read in the paper about the Dodgers trading him to the New York Giants, I didn't understand it at all. But later in years I remembered that he didn't get along well with Walter Alston, who became the Dodger's manager in 1954. There was even a rumor that Alston challenged Jackie to a fight during spring training in 1955.

Jackie was really the main man in the civil rights movement. People don't realize that. Martin Luther King Jr. came to him and asked about his situation and got advice from Jackie before he went out there to spread his message. He talked to Jackie all the time. Jackie was the real civil rights leader because he had to go through it by himself. He didn't have people marching behind him or bodyguards. He had to hold his tongue because he liked to fight a little bit, too. In the Army, he wouldn't sit in the back of the bus and they wanted to give him a dishonorable discharge. But he won his case.

Schemin' and Scammin'

I signed out of high school in June 1956, and got my signing bonus. Signing bonuses were a nice little scheme, a nice little scam.

If you signed for anything over $4,000, you had to go to the major leagues right away and you had to stay there for at least two years. So then a team's advice to the player was, "Well, if you do that, you lose that experience of going to the minor leagues. So the best thing I can do is give you $4,000."

What was I going to do? At the time I signed, I didn't know about under-the-table money. The Dodgers didn't give me anything under the table. But I heard that my counterpart, Bobby Aspromonte, who signed at the same time as I did, got a little money under the table. He also got to go to Japan with the team that year on its tour.

Not me. I got $4,000. That went straight to my stomach. I weighed 194 pounds and went up to 204 in a week. I ate a whole bunch of steaks. Really, though, the $4,000 went to help my family. And I went to the minors. Back then, the minors went from Class D and up and it took four, five, six years to make it to the big leagues because there were only eight teams in each league. The Dodgers knew how to play the game, so I was anxious to get to the big leagues.

Baseball As Homework

I took with me to the Dodgers the knowledge of the game I learned on the sandlots of Brooklyn. I truly learned the intricacies of the game when I played for the Brooklyn Bisons as a 16 year old. It was a Kiwanis League team and the coach, Clarence Irving, was the only black manager in the league. We would go to the parade grounds behind Prospect Park in Brooklyn for team meetings and then he would give us homework. But it wasn't on the three R's. It was on baseball—hitting the cut-off man, when to drop a sacrifice bunt, how to correctly field a ground ball. It made us actually learn the game instead of just playing it and we were better players because of it.

The Bisons made it to the 1955 state championship in Cooperstown where we played a team called the Watertown Johnnies. They were beating us, 5-2, until they started talking trash. We had an ethnic team and they knew it. Our first baseman and right fielder were Italian, our second baseman and shortstop were black, our third baseman was Jewish and I was in left field. They started calling us names like "Wop" and "Kike" and then they called me "Sambo." All that did was make us mad and it gave us the inspiration to come back. We ended up beating them, 7-5.

This Is Easy

Nobody taught me how to hit. It was just something that came naturally to me. When I was nine years old, I started playing fast-pitch softball. That ball comes at you real fast and the pitcher is very close. So when I began playing baseball, it seemed like the ball was coming at me real slow. I thought, "Shoot, this is easy."

As I got older, I had to learn how to pull the ball. Even when I got in the big leagues I would watch other guys and take some tips from them. I never stopped learning. I used to watch the Chicago Cubs' Billy Williams take batting practice, just to see how he would pull the ball. We called him "The Whistler" because that's how the bat sounded when he was up there raking it, pulling the ball into the corner.

2

LIFE IN THE MINORS

Away from Home

The first place the Dodgers sent me was to Hornell, New York. I had never been homesick until I got there. I mean, sure, I was still in New York, but it was far enough from home that I missed Brooklyn. It was three or four hours away.

I just wanted to play ball. We were playing in what was called the Pony League. That was the first time I played under the lights. It was strange. It seemed like the ball just came up on me really fast. I batted .325 in my first professional season.

My teammates weren't young guys. They were pretty old. Our second baseman, Joey Lawrence, had a pregnant wife, but he was the one who had the morning sickness. He kept throwing up. He was sick all day long. He'd come to the ballpark looking all pale so I would ask him, "What's wrong with you, man?" What made it even funnier was that his wife was eating hot dogs and all kinds of stuff at the games.

In the town of Hornell, J.W. Lockett and a shoeshine guy were the only blacks. Lockett was a pitcher who hurt his arm and the Dodgers got rid of him, which I thought was terrible. After they cut him, the next spring training I went in and said, "He's a good guy, he's the breadwinner of his whole family because he didn't have a dad. He's a real good worker, a hell of a guy. If he's healthy, you'll really like him." I was almost in tears I liked him so much.

The general manager said, "Son, you've got a lot of guts, but you better mind your own business and let me do my business. You're young. Now get out of here."

J.W. turned out okay, though. He ended up playing professional football as a running back for the Dallas Cowboys and the Baltimore Colts.

On to Kokomo

I was very gratified to have Pete Reiser as my manager in Kokomo, Indiana, because he was like a father figure to me. I was so young and he kept me in check. He was tough, though. As a player with the Dodgers, Pete hit .343 in 1941 and won the batting title, but was known mostly for his hardnosed play in the outfield. He often knocked himself out by crashing into the unpadded concrete walls of Ebbets Field. He went to Los Angeles as a coach on Walt Alston's staff from 1960 to 1964, but before that he cut his managing teeth in the minors.

We didn't play so good one game. We had an eight-hour bus ride on the way back from Iowa and didn't get back to Indiana until eight o'clock the following morning. On the ride home Pete made an announcement: "As soon as you guys get your clothes and go home," he said, "come back by 11. We're going to have a workout. And I'm going to warn you, don't have any breakfast."

So we were like, "What the hell is he talking about?" There were only 16 players on our roster in Class D. We had one utility player and six pitchers plus the position players. So we came back and he had all of us running. While the pitchers were running in the outfield we had to run home to first, come back and then run home to second, then come back and run home to third and then go all the way around. That was kind of hard.

Meanwhile, the pitchers are running out in the outfield. Pete took a break from yelling at us to yell at them, "Faster than that!" And all of a sudden I heard somebody go, "Blahhhh." About three guys just barfed on the field out there. I guess that's why he told us not to eat because it was going to come back up anyway.

Running Wild

I guess all that running helped after all. I was flying around the bases in those days and I didn't even know how to run. I mean, I didn't know how to run the bases correctly, but I still stole 68 bases to lead the league that year. And I also led the league in hitting with a .357 average. I was really proud of my accomplishments, especially all the steals.

Later in my major league career, when I was in the American League, we were playing the Washington Senators, and this young guy, Ed Stroud, came up to me during a game and smiled at me. He said, "I got you, baby." I didn't know what he was talking about but he kept on. "I got you in the Midwest League, baby. I got 70, baby."

He was talking about stolen bases. He broke my record and he literally chased me down to tell me about it. He was real proud of himself. And he should have been. He ended up stealing 72 bases in the big leagues in a career that stretched over six seasons.

A Learning Experience

In Kokomo, I lived with a lady named Mama Lutie Brown. My roommates included Teacup Wheeler and Napoleon Savinon. I guess we used to raid her refrigerator because she had to put a lock on it. One time we were drinking vodka and man, I was throwing up all over the place. She took care of me.

She said, "You're a young boy. You can't drink like that, son, and play baseball." She talked real slow.

Teacup was hilarious. His first name was really Burbon and he had this one tooth that stuck out in the front. When he was laughing, it looked like he was crying.

We all felt like crying one night when we were on a road trip in Dubuque, Iowa. After a game, we were walking down the street and we came across a woman walking a little boy. He was about seven years old. He saw us and then he pulled on the lady's dress and pointed at us and asked, "Mom, is that what you call a nigger?" We didn't know what to say or if we should say anything, so we just kept on walking.

Strange Bedfellows

One time, Tea Cup, Napoleon and I stayed out real late, past curfew. When we came in, Pete Reiser was in my bed. He said, "You're late. Listen, you're going to get fined, but don't wake me up. See you in the morning." Then he turned over, pulled the covers up—my covers—and got comfortable. He slept the rest of the night there, in my bed. I was upset, and I said, "C'mon, man, where am I going to sleep?" He said, "I don't give a damn."

He slept in my bed all night and I had to sleep on the floor. It was great, though. I was a baby, a young fella.

Service Denied

In Kokomo, I hung around with Willie Ivory. If it wasn't for him, I would have been hurt. At a restaurant one time, we waited 45 minutes for someone to notice us. And the cook had a cleaver. He

As a player, Pete Reiser was a hard-headed competitor who oftentimes knocked himself out running into the unpadded concrete outfield walls at Ebbets Field. But as a minor league manager and big-league coach, Pete was like a daddy to me. Courtesy of the Los Angeles Dodgers held it down at his side, just in case we started something, just in case I started acting a fool.

Willie said, "Let's get out of here because they're not going to serve us."

So I said, "What do you mean they're not going to serve us?" I was a young and crazy kid from Brooklyn. "You've got to be out of your mind. They'll serve us," I said. But they didn't.

Like a Daddy

Coming up through the minor leagues I made friendships that lasted throughout my whole career and my life. I had one such a relationship with Pete Reiser.

During spring training with the Dodgers, Pete used to ask me, "Why are you always smiling at the plate?"

I said, "I don't know. I just smile. I'm young and crazy."

He said, "The next time you smile, and you have the bat in your hand, I'm fining you $500."

That took me by surprise so I said, "But Pete, I only make $350...a month!"

He was like a daddy to me. But the funny thing about Pete getting on me about smiling all the time was that it happened so early in my career. Later on I was known as a stoic, unemotional ballplayer. I just did my job. I wasn't like Jose Lima, the one-time Dodgers pitcher who was so demonstrative on the mound. Off the field, maybe I was boisterous. But on the field, I didn't want to be a hot dog, a person who tries to get attention. I just wanted to be very quiet and do my job and maybe the pitchers wouldn't throw at me. In those days they threw at you a lot. And I didn't want to get fined by Pete Reiser, either.

The South Rises Again

After my stop at Kokomo, I went to Victoria, Texas, for the 1958 season. It was a combination team because half the team was comprised of the old Shreveport team, which had dissolved, and half was the Dodgers. So I went from Class D to Double A, which was a big jump in those days.

But before I went, Dodgers general manager Buzzie Bavasi pulled me aside and said, "Listen, son, you're going to be in the South. You can expect some things that are a little bit different than New York City. So you have to deal with it and mature."

They sent a guy with me to be my roommate. He was a little older and was supposed to, I guess, keep me alive. His was a Puerto Rican named Roberto Vargas. But he left after a month. He was just gone. He had pitched in 25 games for the Milwaukee Braves in 1955 so he was a veteran. But after he left, I was there by myself the rest of the year.

I felt like Jackie Robinson all over again. I went through a lot of hell. In Victoria I could hear everything and everybody because it was only a 5,000-seat stadium. If I did something good, they'd say stuff like, "That's our nigger. He's doing all right." But if I didn't do so well, I definitely heard about it. I went through that stuff all the time.

Out of the Box

There was another black guy in the league who was around 40 years old who played on another team. His name was Nat Peoples. He was the fastest thing in the league—even at that age. He was kicking our butt. I was playing in right field and I could tell that the fans wanted to yell something at him but they couldn't, because he was kicking our butt.

When he batted, his back foot would go out of the batter's box. It would just creep out, slowly but surely to the point where his foot was completely out of the box when he made contact with the ball. Because the stadium was so small and so quiet, I could hear this one fan from behind home plate say, "Mr. Umpire, could you please keep the nigger's foot in the box?"

I was laughing like crazy because Peoples was hitting doubles and triples and stealing all these bases. And that's all the crowd could say. "Could you please keep the nigger's foot in the box?" I was rolling.

There was nothing else they could pick on him for, so they went with his foot coming out of the box.

Dealing with Ignorance

One time a ground ball came to me in the outfield and it went under my legs. It went all the way to the fence and I went to chase it down, running like crazy. As I was running for it, I heard, "Nigger, keep going, jump over the damn fence and don't come back." I could hear that as clear as a bell. At the time, I just laughed. I thought it was funny. What else could I do? But later, it gave me more inspiration to hit the ball well, to go out there and just beat the ball because that kind of thing just gave me more fuel.

Every once in a while, a visiting team would say racial things, and since I was the only black on the team, I'd look over there into their dugout, just to let them know I heard them. And they'd say, "Yeah, I'm talking to you." Man, I got so mad I just wanted to answer by going over there and saying, "Well, I'm here. Ain't nothing between us but air. You want me to blow that away?" That's what I wanted to do, but I couldn't do that. I knew I had to just deal with that kind of stuff.

When the Dodgers signed me, they didn't say it would be like what Jackie went through. But they did say, "Look, you're going to be up against segregation and you're going to have to deal with it." They were testing me. They didn't have to send me there to Texas, did they? I think I passed their test.

Deep in the Heart of Texas

While the fans and other teams would say and do racist things toward me, the people on my team took care of me. One of my teammates was Don Miles, another prospect with the Dodgers. Don was so strong, he would put water in a bottle, fill it up about three-quarters full, and then hit the top of the bottle with the palm of his hand and the bottom of the bottle would explode—it would pop right off.

He ended up playing eight games for the Dodgers in 1958, after they moved to Los Angeles. His best move, though, was probably marrying one of the daughters of the owners of our team, the Victoria Rosebuds.

We were good friends. One time, he said, "Let's go to a movie." I said, "I can't go to a movie, man." I couldn't even go to a movie in town due to segregation, and he didn't even realize that because he didn't see me for my skin color. He just saw me as a teammate. He didn't care. He would break the law in a minute if he didn't think it was right.

I didn't go into town very often. There were things to do instead. I played games every day so I didn't have much time to do anything else. I liked the people. Every place I went was a new experience for me and I enjoyed my time there.

North of the Border

My wrist was injured when they called me up to Montreal for the end of the 1958 season. I was hitting about .315 at the time; I ended up hitting .304 in Texas. I don't recall how I injured my wrist, though. When I first got up to Montreal, I was sneaking into the whirlpool and the manager, Clay Bryant, saw me and said, "What's wrong with him?" One of the guys was trying to be cool, trying to help me out by downplaying my injury, and said, "I don't know, I think he hurt his wrist or something." I can still hear Clay saying, "Then what the hell did they bring him up here for?" Oh, man. I felt so bad.

But I got in a couple of games, and this particular team won the International League championship. Sparky Anderson played second base. I hit .308 for the 14 games I played there. Tommy Lasorda was on that team as a coach and player. He was 18-6 as a pitcher. He was a great minor league pitcher with a really good curveball.

"It was the last day of the season and we had already clinched the night before so I played first base that game," Lasorda recalled many years later. "I hit a home run and Tommy Davis hit a home run. What a way to end the season."

It was. What made it all the more memorable, though, was that because we had clinched, most of the guys were drunk from partying and carrying on the night before. One guy, Bob Lennon, fell on his face rounding first.

It was a good experience living in Montreal. Especially after being in the South. The way I saw it, Montreal didn't have that many black people anyhow so they could afford to be nice to us and treat us right. I always thought, though, that if 200,000 of us came there, all of a sudden they'd be like, "Hey, wait just a minute." But they treated me awfully well.

I even learned a little bit of French. I stayed with a little old lady who lived above a grocery store and I used to ask her, "Comment allez-vous?" And she'd say back to me, "Tres bien." Or vice versa. I would have liked to have lived there a while longer. I felt so comfortable there.

I made a name for myself with a bat in my hand and at the plate as a hitter, but no one could deny my flair for the dramatic in the outfield at Spokane, at least not when the photo was staged. Courtesy of the Los Angeles Dodgers

3

MY EARLY YEARS
IN THE SHOW

Best Seat in the House

After having such a good minor-league year in 1959, I was hoping that I could at least get called up to the big club, the Dodgers, for the last part of the season. I did, and I watched them win. I had a great seat, probably the best seat in the house. But before I got there, they had an amazing midseason turnaround. They were middling about in fifth place in June. After finishing in seventh place the year before, Walter Alston was on the hot seat. It seemed like Alston was always in trouble. Maybe that was because the owner, Mr. Walter O'Malley, only gave out one-year contracts to his managers.

There was talk that the players were on the verge of a mutiny, because a lot of them wanted Pee Wee Reese to take over as manager less than a year after playing his last game. He became a coach for Alston instead, and then the Dodgers changed their personality midstream when Maury Wills, a shortstop who had been in the minor leagues for more than eight years, and two rookie pitchers, Larry Sherry and Roger Craig, combined with Don Drysdale and Sandy

Koufax to take center stage and propel the Dodgers to 86 victories.

At the end of the regular season we—and I say *we* because I was in uniform at the end of the year—were tied with the Milwaukee Braves and had to play a best-of-three playoff series with them to claim the National League pennant and get into the World Series against the Chicago White Sox. They were called the "Go-Go Sox" because of their flashy style of play.

Because I was a late-season call-up I wasn't able to play in the playoff, but still I felt like a part of the team. The Dodgers went to Milwaukee and beat the Braves, 3-2, in Game 1, courtesy of John Roseboro's home run and Larry Sherry's dominant relief pitching. Game 2 was at the Coliseum and that infamous net in left field helped us out.

The Braves and their starting pitcher, Lew Burdette, took a 5-2 lead into the ninth inning when Wally Moon, Duke Snider and Gil Hodges all hit singles to load the bases. Norm Larker followed up with a high fly to left that hit the screen and Wally and Duke both scored easily as Gil made it to third. The tying run was 90 feet away.

The Braves then brought in right-handed reliever Don McMahon, who would become a scout for the Dodgers in the 1980s. Sadly, he died of a heart attack after pitching batting practice to the team at Dodger Stadium on July 22, 1987. On this day, though, he retired Roseboro, and the Braves brought in Hall of Famer Warren Spahn, who was normally a starter, to face Carl Furillo. Carl's sacrifice fly scored Gil and the game went to extra innings. The Dodgers had to use Sandy Koufax, Clem Labine and Stan Williams in extra innings to hold off the Braves, and they worked out fine by keeping the Braves off the scoreboard. What made their performance all the more impressive was how wild that pitching staff was that year. It set still-standing Los Angeles Dodgers records by hitting 51 batters and walking 614 others.

We clinched the pennant in the bottom of the 12th when Hodges scored from second base on Felix Mantilla's throwing error. The final score was Dodgers, six, Braves, five.

The 1959 World Series would mark the first time that the Dodgers would play a team other than the Yankees in the Fall Classic since 1920. That's when Brooklyn lost to the Cleveland Indians, five games to two, in what was then a best-of-nine format.

Bring on the Go-Go White Sox

In only their second year in Los Angeles the Dodgers were in the World Series. It was a memorable season, one that included an exhibition game against the New York Yankees on May 7 that honored Roy Campanella. Campy was a three-time National League Most Valuable Player for the Brooklyn Dodgers who did not get a chance to play in L.A. because he was paralyzed in a car accident on January 27, 1958. The night of the tribute, a crowd of 93,103 filled the Coliseum. Pee Wee Reese pushed Campy to home plate in his wheelchair, and they turned the lights off and the fans lit matches to give the stadium an otherworldly glow.

Big crowds were the norm that year, especially in the World Series, when crowds of more than 92,000 came to Games 3, 4 and 5 at the Coliseum to set attendance records. By the time of the first ever Fall Classic game in Los Angeles, the 1959 World Series was tied after the Dodgers and White Sox split the first two games in Chicago. The White Sox pounded Roger Craig in Game 1, 11-0, and Ted Kluszewski hit two homers for them. In Game 2, Charlie Neal followed in Ted's footsteps by going deep twice, and Larry Sherry relieved Johnny Podres in the third inning and gave up one run in the Dodgers' 4-3 win.

The Dodgers won the first two World Series games in L.A. with a massive, record-breaking crowd on hand. For Game 3, 92,394

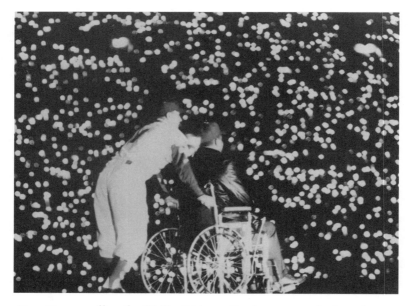

Roy Campanella, the Hall of Fame Catcher, never had a chance to play in L.A. because he was paralyzed in a car accident the winter before the team's relocation. Still, L.A. honored him when Pee Wee Reese pushed Campy's wheelchair to home plate with fans at the Coliseum lighting matches for him with the stadium lights off.
Courtesy of the Los Angeles Dodgers

were in attendance. Drysdale pitched into the eighth inning, Sherry came in out of the bullpen, and Furillo's two-run pinch-hit single in the seventh was the difference as we won, 3-1.

Game 4, played before an even bigger crowd of 92,650, was tied at four-all before Hodges homered to right field in the eighth inning to win it, 5-4. We were one win away from a championship. And we could have celebrated it at the Coliseum. The Go-Go White Sox would not go away, though.

Our bats were asleep in Game 5, even if the record crowd of 92,706 was electric, and even though Sandy Koufax pitched a gem, we lost 1-0 because Bob Shaw threw a shutout at us. Having to go back to the Windy City, you'd think some of the wind would have been taken out our sails. But it wasn't. The Dodgers jumped on Early Wynn early on and built an 8-0 lead. With Sherry relieving Podres and pitching lights out, we won, 9-3.

It did not seem fair that the Dodgers won a World Series in just their second year in Los Angeles when it took Brooklyn 66 years to win its one and only championship. But that's the way it went, thanks to so many different heroes. Chuck Essegian played in only 24 regular-season games that year but he had two huge pinch-hit home runs. Charlie Neal batted. 370 and had six RBIs, and Larry Sherry was named the MVP with two wins and two saves.

Baseball, championship baseball, was here to stay in Los Angeles. They could never take that away. They treated us like royalty on opening day in 1960. We had a parade through the streets of downtown L.A. that ended on the steps of City Hall with a meeting with the mayor. By winning their second ever World Series in just their second year in L.A., only four years after claming their first championship, the Dodgers became the first team to win world titles on both coasts of the United States. They had won the 1955 World Series against the Yankees when Johnny Podres, as a 23 year old, won Game 7, 2-0, for Brooklyn's only World Series title. Johnny always considered himself a better pitcher when the stakes were the greatest.

Bringing Baseball to L.A.

Professional baseball was not entirely new to Southern California. They had been playing it here for many years in the Pacific Coast League with the old Los Angeles Angels and the Hollywood Stars. It was just that Major League Baseball was new.

Vin Scully, the Dodgers' Hall of Fame announcer, made the trip from Brooklyn. He said the organization was at a crossroads when it moved to Los Angeles in 1958.

"They had won the World Series in '55 and they had won the pennant in '56 but when they came out here in '58, they knew they had an old team," Vin said. "So the big decision by management was, 'Do we bring an old team out there that's not going to go anywhere? Or do we bring a lot of kids out there and start out fresh?' And they were smart, they brought out the old team. Because the people here at least knew the names—Duke Snider, Carl Furillo, Gil Hodges, Pee Wee Reese—even though they couldn't play very well. People related to them. That was in '58, [when they] finished seventh, two games out of last place. They were hopeless. That's what made winning the World Series in '59 so surprising."

Playing baseball in a football stadium was a novelty, sure, but it did not keep the crowd away as 78,672 came to the Los Angeles Memorial Coliseum for Opening Day on April 18, 1958, when the Dodgers met the new San Francisco Giants. Courtesy of the Los Angeles Dodgers

They were indeed hopeless that first year. The Dodgers were on the losing end so often in that first season, and there was a joke going around that asked what the "L.A." on the front of the Dodger cap stood for. The punchline was that it stood for "Lost Again."

After Carl Erskine made history by throwing the first pitch in Los Angeles Dodgers history—he threw a called strike at the San Francisco Giants' Jim Davenport before a Coliseum crowd of 78,672 on April 18, 1958—the Dodgers won the home opener, 6-5, and Dick Gray hit the first ever home run by an L.A. Dodger. But the good vibes were quickly lost. That Dodger team finished 71-83, the Dodgers' poorest season in 14 years and the team's worst winning percentage until 1992, when they went 63-99. That first L.A. pitching staff had a rough go of it at the Coliseum with a franchise-record 70 wild pitches, tying the record set in 1894. But the fans loved them. Maybe it was because not everything on the field was negative. That first L.A. Dodgers team also set a franchise record by turning 198 double plays. I guess that was because the pitching staff had allowed so many opposing runners on base.

To the Moon

Vin Scully also thought that a winter deal was the key to the Dodgers' surprising run to the World Series a year after moving to L.A.

"They had traded a young outfielder named Gino Cimoli," Vin said. "Some people thought he was going to be another Joe DiMaggio. He was Italian and handsome and he could play the outfield defensively. But he never could hit. So they traded Gino Cimoli to the St. Louis Cardinals for a left-handed hitting outfielder named Wally Moon. And Wally Moon is the guy who was hitting balls over the screen in left field and into the screen and Moon had a huge year and that was one of the reasons they won the pennant and the World Series."

They called those hits Moon Shots because of the high arc of the ball when it approached that screen. Wally had an even better individual season in 1961, the Dodgers' final season at the Coliseum. That year he set the Los Angeles Dodgers record for highest batting average by a left-handed hitter by batting .328. He still holds that mark. Wally is also in the record book as the last man to score a run at the Coliseum. He crossed home plate in the 13th inning to give us a 3-2 win over the Chicago Cubs on September 20, 1961. I don't know who was happier to leave the Coliseum, the Dodger hitters or the Dodger pitchers.

Crowds and Transistor Radios

Playing baseball in a football stadium was one thing. Watching it in such a strange setting was another animal entirely. Vin Scully is credited with teaching Southern California all about the game of baseball, the same way the late Chick Hearn is thought to have taught L.A. about basketball when the Lakers moved to Los Angeles in 1960.

"I remember the crowds more than anything, and transistor radios," Vin said. ". . . People brought transistor radios and we could hear it all over the place. We had the crowd sing "Happy Birthday" to Frank Secory, one of the umpires.

"It was big time at the Coliseum. You had 79 rows of seats that went straight up and you had people sitting at the very top. And although the fans knew Willie Mays and they knew Stan Musial, they didn't know the rank-and-file players at all, so they brought the transistor radio to get information. . . . Because of the number of transistor radios in the Coliseum, there was a lot of feedback coming in, and the engineer went crazy. We had a lot of fun with it. It's always dangerous to play with the crowd so we didn't do it much."

The Dodgers initially considered playing at Wrigley Field in South Central Los Angeles. But it only had seats for 25,000 fans, and it was a launching pad. When the Angels played there in their expansion season of 1961, they gave up 248 home runs in just 81 games. It was a great setting for the *Home Run Derby* TV show of the 1960s. Just not so good for Major League Baseball games.

0 for 1

I was in Portland, Oregon, on a road trip with the Spokane Indians when the Dodgers called me up at the end of the 1959 regular season. I was happy. I knew I was going up, but I didn't know whether I was going to play or not. Well I did. Kind of. I got up one time . . . and I struck out. Against Marshall Bridges. A brother. I'll never forget his name—Marshall Bridges. A left-handed brother from St. Louis. I just thought, "You could have done better than that for a young brother like me. Shoot, I'm trying to stay, man. You've got to be kidding."

I didn't say that, though. I just thought it and looked at him. I think he caught my drift, though, because he just shrugged, like, "Hey, man, I've got a job to do, too."

And because only the guys on the big club got rings, I missed out that first year on some hardware. That was okay, though, I'd get my own in 1963.

Making the Club

It was early in the 1960 season and I got my first professional hit against the St, Louis Cardinals' Ron Kline on April 14 at the Coliseum. Ron actually came and played with the Dodgers the next year. We beat the Cardinals that day, 3-2, so I felt pretty good about contributing to the win, even if my hit was just an infield single to the shortstop. And even though I had made the Dodgers' Opening Day roster, I was still scared that I would be sent down to the minors at any moment. But after a game in Chicago when the season wasn't yet 12 games old, Walt Alston came up to me in the clubhouse at Wrigley Field. He said to me, "Don't be so nervous, you've got this team made. Just be yourself." I was really happy to hear that and I got really comfortable after that.

I didn't play much, but I did pretty good for the time I was in the lineup, hitting .276 with 11 home runs and 44 RBIs in 110 games. I was young, and I just wanted to play; I was happy to be there. The Dodgers tried to put me at third base but I threw like an outfielder. So it was out to left field for me.

I got to see Norm Larker go after the batting championship in 1960. He batted .323 but was just beaten out by the Pittsburgh Pirates' Dick Groat, who hit .325. There was this controversial play in left field. The guy caught a one-hopper off Norm's bat and the umpire called it a catch—an out. With that hit Norm, who batted .275 for his career, would have won the batting title that season. Only one Dodger has won a batting title since the Dodgers moved to California. Guess who?

Lost in the Netting

I had gone to so many games as a youngster at Ebbets Field that the stadium was like a second home. It was a small stadium, a bandbox, but it was a baseball stadium, no doubt about it. When the Dodgers moved to L.A. in 1958, they had to play on a converted football field at the Los Angeles Memorial Coliseum because Dodger Stadium would not be ready and up and running for another four years. So my first major-league at-bat in 1959, and my first two full seasons in 1960 and 1961, were at the Coliseum, a historical place that had hosted the Olympics in 1932, and would again in 1984. Playing baseball there, though, was strange. There was a bad glare in the day at the Coliseum because the sun set behind home plate. The lights at night weren't all that bright either and kind of gave the field a foggy look to it.

And then there were the dimensions. The left field stands were only 250 feet away from home plate, but they put up a 40-foot-high fence that went 140 feet out to center field to keep the home run count down. And it did. And the left power alley was only 320 feet away, center field was 425 feet deep with a six-foot tall screen and the right-field power alley was a monstrous 440 feet away while the right field foul pole was just 300 feet down the line. Strange dimensions for a strange ballpark. But players adjusted to it.

My two full years there, I hit .276 and .278. I lost a lot of home runs there because I hit a lot of line drives. I had to go like hell to get to first. The ball would come straight down off that netting in left field, and the left fielders, they'd turn around and they could throw it. They had strong arms. Wally Moon, who I eventually replaced in the lineup, made a living hitting looping fly balls off the netting. In 1960 and 1961, I hit 11 and then 15 home runs in each season. It should have been more like 17 and 22 because I hit a couple of goodies at home that would have gone out anywhere else. But that's the way it was. We all had to deal with it.

Ron Fairly had a unique take on it because he knew what to expect at the Coliseum having played there in his college days.

"Interestingly enough, the USC team took batting practice there before the Dodgers came out to Los Angeles," Ron said. "Even with the left-field foul pole only 250 feet away, I would still come up 10 feet short. Throughout my entire career, regardless of what the dimensions were, I was always about 10 feet short."

That's what you call "Warning Track Power."

The Coliseum Robs The Duke

Edwin Donald Snider—or simply, Duke—was known as the Duke of Flatbush when the Dodgers called Brooklyn home. But he was a pauper for power after the Dodgers moved West and began playing in the Coliseum. The transformed football field and track stadium robbed Duke of much of his clout, even if he was a native of Los Angeles. In Duke's defense, right field was 1,000 miles away. How the hell was he going to hit anything out there? After hitting 40 home runs in 1957, the Dodgers' final year in Brooklyn, the left-handed-hitting Duke went deep just 15 times in 1958, the Dodgers' first year on the West Coast.

It was obvious that Duke was never truly comfortable enough in L.A. to have the kinds of seasons he had in Brooklyn, when fans used to argue over the best center fielder in New York—the Giants' Willie Mays, the Yankees' Mickey Mantle or the Duke. What made Duke's power shortage in LA all the more surprising was that it came after he had five straight seasons of 40 or more homers. In his last five seasons in Brooklyn, Duke averaged more than 41 homers. In five seasons in L.A., Duke averaged less than 15 homers. He is still, however, the franchise's all-time home run king with 389 career homers, and he also leads in RBIs with 1,271. Duke wasn't the only one hurt by the dimensions of the Coliseum, since no Dodger ever hit more than 14 home runs there in a single season.

Playing the Net

Playing defense at the Coliseum was a different animal as well, especially with the strange dimensions and, of course, with that netting in left. It wasn't like having to play balls off the Green Monster in Boston's Fenway Park. That wall is hard, and the balls bounce off it real quick in every direction. The netting at the Coliseum was soft, so the balls just died. The ball would hit it on the fly, the net would absorb it and the ball would just fall straight down. You just had to get right under it. You were only 250 feet away anyhow, so if it was a line drive, you could get it and turn around and try to throw somebody out at first base. There weren't any standards there, either, for the ball to ricochet off.

I played a lot of centerfield, too. I made one of the best catches that nobody ever saw. It was similar to the one that everybody remembers Willie Mays making, that over-the-shoulder grab of Vic Wertz's 460-foot shot while running towards the center field fence at the old Polo Grounds in Game 1 of the 1954 World Series. It was foggy one night, like it can get in the Coliseum, and someone hit a drive to center and I ran out into the fog and made the catch over my shoulder. Just like Willie. The umpire didn't even know what was happening. No one saw it except for these 10 guys sitting out there in the stands by themselves, way out there. They started clapping and yelling and stuff so the umpire knew I made the catch. A major league game, and only 10 guys were sitting out there. Granted, it was more than 400 feet away from home plate.

Dodger Blue Bloodline

The 1960 and 1961 Dodger teams were a combination of the old and the new. In 1960 we didn't do anything as a team. We had a winning record of 82-72, but we finished in fourth place. In 1961 we were close. We were 89-65 and took second place, four games behind the Cincinnati Reds. There was still a Brooklyn feel to the team, but those players were getting older, or in the cases of Gil Hodges, Carl Furillo and Clem Labine, they were being boxed out and pushed aside.

Carl Erskine, who threw the first pitch in Los Angeles Dodgers history, had retired during the 1959 season. Three years after moving to L.A., the only Brooklyn players remaining on the roster were Duke Snider, Jim Gilliam, Charley Neal, Don Drysdale, Sandy Koufax and Johnny Podres. I was part of the young guns who were coming aboard and becoming regulars, along with Frank Howard, Maury Wills, Ron Fairly and Willie Davis.

I was a young boy when I came up, and the guys who were on the team already were my heroes, and here I was playing with some of them. I grew up watching guys like Gil Hodges, Clem Labine, Carl Erskine, Roy Campanella and Don Newcombe. Talk about a dream come true. I was now officially part of the Dodger Blue bloodline, something that reaches out far into baseball. Think about it: Between 1960 and 1980 most teams had a Dodger either in their front office or a manager or coach who was a former Dodger. Don Zimmer, Frank Howard, Norm Sherry, Dick Williams, Sparky Anderson, Bobby Lillis, Johnny Podres. There were just so many guys from that time period. You wouldn't believe how many people from the Dodgers organization infiltrated other organizations.

The Dodgers knew how to play ball. And I was just young enough and crazy enough to be just shy of cocky. When we were playing the Pittsburgh Pirates in my rookie year, Roger Craig came in to pitch from the bullpen, and after his inning, when he came back into the dugout, I told Roger, "If I get in this game, I'll win it for you." Well, I got in the game, and I won it with a home run in the 11th inning.

Get It? Dodger Stadium Opens

Dodger Stadium opened for business on April 10, 1962, and it was the first privately financed stadium since The House that Ruth Built, Yankee Stadium, opened in 1923. But Dodger Stadium's arrival did not come without a few hiccups along the way. The opening was threatened by heavy rains two months before the start of the season. The rains caused a reported $500,000 damage to the stadium and they had to hustle to get it ready for opening day. In fact, because it took so long for Dodger Stadium to be built, there had even been rumors that Walter O'Malley was threatening to go back to Brooklyn if Dodger Stadium did not open.

It was ready for the 1962 season opener, but unfortunately we weren't ready as a team. In front of a crowd of 52,564, and with Johnny Podres pitching for us, we had an inauspicious debut. We lost to the Cincinnati Reds, 6-3.

And that's not all that went wrong that day. What looked like a swarm of moths hovered over the stands, bothering the fans. The foul poles were mistakenly placed in foul territory. And someone forgot to put water fountains throughout the stadium for the fans. A lot of conspiracy theorists claimed that it was a ploy by Walter O'Malley to make the fans spend more money, because if they were thirsty, they'd have to start buying soft drinks and beer. At the Coliseum, the Dodgers could not sell beer, so that would be a big money-maker right there.

Ron Fairly also remembers the stadium grounds crew having to put food coloring on the grass to make it all look green because there were some dead spots in the outfield.

"Mr. O'Malley addressed us in a team meeting before the game and said, 'There are a few kinks, but we will not criticize the stadium,'" Ron said. "He made that abundantly clear. 'We will not criticize the stadium. Get it?'" Oh yeah, we got it.

We also got a sense that Dodger Stadium was the ultimate pitcher's park. Gone were the days of the Dodgers being built on power hitters who loved to muscle up and go deep.

"It was easier to hit the ball over the right-field fence at the Coliseum, which was almost 400 feet away, than it was to hit it out of Dodger Stadium," Ron said.

And he spoke from experience. In the first two years that we called Dodger Stadium home, Ron belted just five home runs at

Chavez Ravine, compared to the 21 he hit on the road during that same timeframe.

"There were very, very few right-handed batters—I mean you can count them on one hand—who hit a ball into those seats in right-centerfield," Ron added. "Frank Robinson did it. I don't know that Willie Mays did. Dick Allen may have done it and Frank Howard. That's about it. It just didn't go. But now that they've moved home plate out 15 feet and as hard as the ball is today, it jumps out."

It didn't jump out for us that day. But the second game at Dodger Stadium was much better. Sandy Koufax started for us and we beat the Reds, 6-2, and Jim Gilliam was the first Dodger to hit a home run in Dodger Stadium.

Going Deep in the Ravine

When the Dodgers came from Brooklyn, they were a power-hitting team. After all, they played in a bandbox of a stadium at Ebbetts Field. It didn't take long for the Dodgers to become a team known for its pitching, though, after the move to Dodger Stadium. But my personal power numbers went up at Dodger Stadium, even with the symmetrical, but still so big stadium dimensions. I hit a lot of line drive-type home runs. It was the way I hit anyhow. I loved the field and I hit 17 home runs that first year in 1962, and it was the Dodger Stadium record until 1974. That's when Jimmy Wynn, the Toy Cannon, broke it. Gary Sheffield broke his record for home runs at Dodger Stadium with 23 in 2000, and Adrian Beltre tied it in 2004. But don't forget, the fence was farther back when I played, too. They brought the plate up a little bit, about 15 feet. So my home runs were longer. That's what I tell myself anyhow.

Sharing Taj O'Malley

Not too many people remember that Dodger Stadium wasn't always known as Blue Heaven by everyone. We called it that, and our fans called it that, but in 1962, the same year "Taj O'Malley" opened, the Los Angeles Angels shared Dodger Stadium with us and they referred to it simply as Chavez Ravine, after the name of the area in which it was built. The Angels didn't move to Anaheim and open up their own stadium in Orange County, about 30 miles down the freeway, until 1965. So for three years the Angels were our neighbors, even though they were treated like stepchildren to some degree. For instance, their offices were located in a back corner, near the hitting cage, deep in the bowels of Dodger Stadium. Way down there, man. We'd walk by every day going to our clubhouse and just think, "Wow, that's the Angels' office? Shit, that's small."

Ron Fairly remembers the Dodgers getting their money's worth from the Halos, though.

"The Dodgers billed the Angels for everything," Ron said. "I remember they made them pay for all the toilet paper in their clubhouse. Walter O'Malley ended up getting into Mr. Autry's pocket a little bit over the lease and everything over Dodger Stadium."

That may be true, but I tell you, you could get into Mr. Autry's pockets. His left pocket could have bought Dodger Stadium. That's how deep his pockets were. There was no real friction between the Dodger and Angel players, though. They weren't there when we played and we were on the road when they played. Daddy Wags was there, Leon Wagner, and Bo Belinsky, he enjoyed himself. He was out there hanging out and partying with the movie stars. We were always contending for the pennant so we didn't really concern ourselves with the Angels. They had a pretty good team, though, especially for being an expansion team. In fact, they set an expansion team record by winning 70 games in 1961. And in 1962 they were only 10 games behind the Yankees for the American League pennant.

4

DODGER CHARACTERS

Wild Thing

When Sandy Koufax first came up, he was one of those wild lefties. We didn't know if he was going to throw a strike or if he was going to throw the ball over the backstop with his next pitch. He thought of quitting many times and even sold electronics in one off-season. But in 1961 during spring training, Norm Sherry was catching him in a split-squad game, and Sherry suggested to Sandy that he take something off the ball. He wanted Sandy to relax his grip and just throw it in there and let the batters hit it. Turns out they couldn't touch him.

I think Alston leaving him alone and just letting him pitch in the rotation helped his confidence, too. Sandy's a sensitive guy. He was one of those bonus babies who had to be on the major league roster even though he would have been better off pitching in the minor leagues.

Batting Practice? I'll Pass

Later in his career, after he became the best pitcher in baseball, I think he liked for people to think that he was still wild and out of control. It was part of his intimidation factor. He didn't have to hit batters or knock them down to intimidate them. He was in their heads already.

In those days, we didn't have specialized batting practice pitchers like they do today, guys whose only job is to throw batting practice to the batters. Back then, it was the pitchers on staff who threw batting practice, and they did it on their off days. Sandy hated throwing batting practice but, as it was at the time, he had to throw live batting practice once a week. So Sandy kind of reverted to his younger days, catch my drift? He threw so hard that the guys didn't want to get up to the plate to face him. One time, I was up there, and he was so mad that he just threw this crazy pitch at about 100-mph right by me. I just stepped out very calmly and said, "Who's next?" I got out of there. I didn't want none of that.

Koufax the Cager

Sandy Koufax is known as arguably the greatest left-handed pitcher of all time. But he was also a great basketball player. He had a college scholarship to play at the University of Cincinnati. But when he was still in high school at Lafayette High, Sandy outplayed a guy who was an All-American at Duquesne University, Sihugo Green. He was from my old high school in Brooklyn, Boys High, and at Duquesne he led the Dukes to the 1955 NIT title, the only national team title in school history. He had his number 11 jersey retired by the school and played nine years in the NBA with the St. Louis Hawks and the Boston Celtics as a sixth man, before they even had a sixth man. He was that good.

Green was about six foot three, so he was too short to be a big man, and he didn't have the skills to be a point guard, but he was a great ballplayer. He was a winner. When his team would win by 23 points, he'd get three. And when they won by three points, he'd get 23. That's sweet.

But Sandy got him. It was legend in Brooklyn. He played against him in a scrimmage game in high school and outplayed him at Boys High School. I never had a chance to play with Sihugo because he graduated in 1953 and I started at Boys High in '53. Sandy got him, though.

"Tommy and I always had a good relationship," Sandy told a reporter. "He remembers me playing basketball at Boys High. He was a kid. I hate to admit that, because that means that Tommy is younger than me."

With Sandy's ability on the basketball court, it makes you wonder if he would have pursued a professional basketball career had he gotten too frustrated with the Dodgers and quit baseball altogether in those early years.

Any One of You

We were allowed to eat steaks on Sundays. Frank Howard was the only one that could have two because that was the deal, evidently. Oh, man, he ate like crazy. Once he got in his food, he never looked up. He didn't look around. He was eating prison-style, like he was on the clock. He had to shovel in his food to get it all in. He would get two steaks on Sundays and we would just watch him eat and go, "Oh my God."

When Frank first came up to the minor leagues, I was with Spokane and Danny Ozark, one of the coaches, had him come over to meet us at Holman Stadium in Vero Beach during spring training. Frank was a huge man—six foot seven, 255 pounds of muscle.

He played both basketball and baseball in college at Ohio State. He walked over toward our dugout, looked in at us and said, "I'll take on any one of you, or all of you if you want, right now. Right now!" This was our introduction to Frank Howard and we all just looked away and didn't say a word. We just whistled. It was like we were whistling through the graveyard. And he said it again, "I'll take on any one of you guys, whoever wants to come out here." We just thought he was crazy. Nobody went out there. Later on we all laughed because he was actually a big Teddy Bear!

But Frank hit the ball so hard and so far. Sometimes shortstops would jump up and try to catch the ball . . . and the ball hit the fence on the fly. On the fly! He had that kind of spin on it, like a golf ball. I saw him get fooled on a pitch on the outside of the plate and he one-handed it over the center-field fence. I mean, he was strong.

In his first full season with the Dodgers in 1960, he batted .268 with 23 home runs and 77 RBIs in 117 games. I remember one time at Forbes Field in Pittsburgh. It was late in the afternoon of a double-header and it got hazy. Frank hit one so far to left-center, into the haze. Usually the umpire will turn around to run to catch up to the ball until it goes over the fence. This time, the umpire went out and the ball was up in the haze and just disappeared. The umpire turned around and went, "Shit, I know it's a home run because it didn't go foul." He just raised his hand and twirled his finger and announced, "Home run."

The First Big Hurt

We called Stan Williams "Big Hurt." This was some 30 years before Frank Thomas, the huge first baseman and designated hitter for the Chicago White Sox, started going by that nickname. Our Big Hurt, Stan, was so big and strong that Ron Fairly remembers him palming guys by the head with his hand the way you palm a basketball.

"You couldn't get out from underneath it," Ron said. "There was nothing you could do. He had you with his grip."

In the clubhouse Stan used to challenge all the guys to shadow box. I'm just as crazy, so one time I said, "Okay, let's go, Big Hurt." We were in the showers and I was moving and shaking and juking and jiving. I was thinking that I was going to outclass him and have some fun doing it. I thought I was going to show him up. And I would have. But Stan doesn't just shadow box. He really hit me in the stomach with his first punch. Hard! And when I was doubled over, trying to catch my breath, he said, "Okay, that's enough." And he walked away, proud of himself. Oh, man, he was crazy.

On the field he threw just as hard as Sandy did—only with less control if you can imagine that. Talk about scary. He'd hit a guy instead of walking him. He'd hit him with the first pitch and then say, "I didn't want to waste the other three pitches."

Ron said there was a method to Big Hurt's madness when it came to drilling batters.

"Stan had a clause in his contract that with X number of base on balls or fewer, he got like an extra thousand dollars," Ron said. "More than that and he didn't get the bonus. So if he went 3 and 0 on a hitter, he'd drill him, because there was nothing in his contract about hit batsmen. There was no way he was going to throw three strikes in a row."

Not too many guys charged the mound when Big Hurt was up there because he'd put an even bigger hurt on whoever charged him. Sometimes, I think he intimidated the guys in our clubhouse more than the guys in the other dugout. Maybe that was just because we saw him all season long.

Ron could be included in that club: "Stan drilled me in a pepper game one time. We were playing pepper in St. Louis and there was a ball that was inside and I just kind of fouled the ball off a little bit and Larry Sherry walked over and picked it up and tossed it to me under-handed, right at me. And I caught it with my bare hand

and I threw the ball to Stan and I got back up to hit and he turned around and the next pitch hit me right in the ribs. He said, 'You weren't looking for two in a row, were you?' He hit me in the ribs and it hurt and I looked at him and he thought that was funny."

Stan had a sick sense of humor. But what happened when he went to the Yankees was anything but funny to the Bronx Bombers, who referred to him as "Hazard." Ron said the nickname originated was because he was a hazard to be around.

"He ended up spiking Whitey Ford in the foot with his shoe when he had to go to the bathroom," Ron said. "He went into one of the stalls, slipped and spiked Whitey in the stall next to him."

There was more to Stan than Big Hurt, though. He was also a hell of a pitcher. In 1961 he struck out 205 batters, the most strikeouts in the National League by a right-hander. Only Sandy Koufax had more in the league, and he fanned 269 batters.

The Talkative Tommy Lasorda

Tommy Lasorda is another of the great characters and storytellers in Dodger lore. The hall of fame manager, who took over for my manager, Walter Alston, late in the 1976 season and stayed in the Dodger dugout until heart problems forced him to retire in 1996, truly bleeds Dodger blue. He was a teammate of mine in Montreal in the minor leagues and he was a master showman. They loved him in Montreal, and he had some great years for them.

"I sure did," Tommy remembers with a sly grin. "But you know, every time I went to spring training with the Dodgers, they'd tell me, 'You've got to come up with another pitch.' I ended up with 11 pitches, that's how many times they told me to come back with something new." He was a legend in the minor leagues and still is in baseball circles.

Tommy Lasorda became one of the game's greatest ambassadors as a manager. But before that, he was a minor league left-handed pitcher—and legend—in Montreal. We were teammates in Montreal for a brief time—almost as brief as his time in a Brooklyn Dodger uniform.
Courtesy of the Los Angeles Dodgers

Brushed Back by Greatness

Because Tommy has been in the Dodgers organization for so many years, he is a walking encyclopedia of Dodger knowledge. He played with some greats and also managed some greats. But it was when the Dodgers were still in Brooklyn and Tommy was up with the Dodgers for one of his many cups of coffee that Tommy had an ironic brush with true greatness.

"We were leading the league by 12 games at the end of June and I was summoned into the office of Buzzie Bavasi, who was then the general manager of the team," Tommy remembered. "He said, 'I've got bad news.' And I said, 'What's wrong, Buzzie, one of your relatives sick?' He said, 'No. We have to send you back to Montreal.'

"So I'm upset and I said, 'Wait a minute, how in the world? I won 20 games, including the playoffs. What do I have to do to show you and the manager that I can pitch here?' He said, 'I've got a real problem. If you were sitting in this seat, who would you let go?' I swear to God this is a true story. I said, 'Koufax. This guy can't hit a barn door 60 feet away with a baseball and you're telling me you're going to keep him and send me out?'

"Buzzie said, 'Well, the baseball rules provide that if you give a guy over $4,000 for a signing bonus, he must remain on the major league club for two years. Koufax stays and you must go.' So now, I can honestly walk around and say that it took the greatest left-handed pitcher in baseball to knock me off the roster. And I still think they made a mistake.

"What an amazing transformation. If you would have seen this guy, Koufax, on that Brooklyn Dodgers team and then seen him four or five years later, unbelievable."

Returning the Favor

Tommy Lasorda told a reporter that he appreciated the way the great Dodger teams of the early and mid-'60s respected him and treated him. Because while he had been an original Brooklyn Dodger and had pitched in just eight major league games and started once in two years in Brooklyn, we were just young pups when we came up and stuck and we still looked up to him.

"They treated me well," Tommy said.

And maybe that's why he returned the favor when he got into a position where he could return respect.

"I did two things that I'm really proud of," Tommy said. "Number 1, when I became the manager of the Dodgers, I went to Jim Gilliam and I said, 'Jim, all you've ever been around here is a first-base coach. I'm telling you right now, I want you to be my hitting coach. You know more about hitting than any of these sons of a bitches we've ever had here. I played with you, I know it.' His eyes got real big and he said, 'Are you serious?' 'You're Goddamned right I'm serious.' He was my hitting coach my first two full seasons, in 1977 and 1978.

"And then I went to Roy Campanella, and Roxie, his wife, has told me this many times."

Campy, a Hall of Fame catcher, was paralyzed and confined to a wheelchair after a car accident the winter before the Dodgers moved from Brooklyn to Los Angeles.

"I said, 'Roy, there's nothing wrong with your mind,'" remembered Tommy. "'You can't walk, but I want you to be a coach.' And for 19 years he was my catching coach. Oh, he'd come out there the next day after a game and he'd chew those guys' asses out and everything. He coached guys like Steve Yeager, Joe Ferguson and Mike Scioscia. At spring training, I told the players, 'You listen to this guy. Not just in catching, but in every phase of the game.'

"He would have been a hell of a manager. He had enthusiasm, the ability to communicate with people. And he loved the game. He really, truly loved the game. He was a star, but he didn't expect everybody to be a star. A lot of stars, when they became the manager, they couldn't stand when the guys didn't do the job right or when they don't do it the way they would have done it. If he would have become a manager, I think he would have been the best of the bunch at managing. At any rate, I was proud of that. Roxie said to me, 'Tommy, you kept him alive for years.' He'd come to spring training with me and he was late one time. I said, 'Uh uh, Roy, you're fined.' He said, 'Goddammit, Tommy, my battery went out.'"

Campy was talking about the battery on his electric wheelchair.

Love and Hate

Maury Wills was a minor league lifer when he got the call to come up to the Dodgers. He had been in the minors for eight-plus years and had even been sold to the Detroit Tigers for a spring. But they didn't want him so he came back to the Dodger system. Maury was in Spokane with me in 1959 when Don Zimmer was struggling in trying to replace the legendary Pee Wee Reese at shortstop with the big club. So the Dodgers made the call in early June and Maury went from Spokane to L.A. as a 26-year-old rookie. He was the sparkplug for the Dodgers that summer as they rallied and won the World Series.

It was in Spokane that Maury learned to become a switch-hitter. Bobby Bragan suggested it and it turned out great. It was the start of a whole new career for Maury. Then, in 1960, Pete Reiser worked with him and Maury gave credit to Pete for saving his career. Pete was my man but he helped Maury, too. It was just so funny that Maury went to Detroit and they didn't want him and he came back and had the greatest season in 1962. That's when he was the National League MVP.

Maury and I had what you'd call a love-hate relationship—we loved to hate each other. Maybe not quite "hate," but you get the idea. We loved to make fun of each other. Spending so much time with each other in the season and playing so close to each other in the field—Maury at shortstop and me in left field—created many tense, memorable and funny moments. In fact, I created history, if you believe Maury. He credits me, so to speak, with saving lives. Because he says the most dangerous play in baseball is when the batter hits a Texas Leaguer, the short pop fly in no-man's land behind the shortstop. The way Maury tells it, you've got me, the left fielder, who's usually a fairly big guy, and Maury, the little shortstop, "running at each other at full speed on that little flare, and the shortstop's neck is exposed because he's looking back and up for the ball."

"The left fielder, Tommy, he's not looking at anything but the ball and he's coming hard," Maury said. "We could never get that play down because of Tommy's indecision out there. He'd never call the ball or tail off. Nothing. And because of that, I tell my players to let it fall and live to play tomorrow. So Tommy's indecisiveness saved lives. Who knew?"

Strange, I never heard him tell that story to the Seattle Mariners when he was their manager and I was his hitting coach.

Snot in His Nose, Tears in His Eyes

One time before a game in Milwaukee, Maury got on the bus wearing this really loud sweater. Too loud. So I started riding him. "What fire sale did you get that thing at?" I yelled at Maury. The whole team joined in and Maury was getting mad, which made everybody ride him that much harder. He was a little sensitive, I guess, because he always liked to look good, or at least think he was looking good. When we got to County Stadium, Maury took me under the stands, so we would be by ourselves, to talk.

"I had snot in my nose and tears in my eyes," Maury said when re-telling the tale to a reporter. "I pushed Tommy and grabbed him by the collar and challenged him to fight, right then and there. 'C'mon,' I said. 'C'mon and fight me.'"

This was getting pretty heated so I said, "I'm not going to hit you. What would it prove if I beat you? You're a little guy, I'm supposed to beat you. But if you beat me, you better not turn your back. Ever."

I think that just made him more mad. Nothing happened, though, and when we got back to the clubhouse, everybody was like, "Where were you guys?"

If they only knew.

Arguing Without Yelling

Some people say that playing the outfield is the most boring job in baseball because relatively few balls are hit out there. The outfielder does have to stay awake in case the ball is hit to him, but it's true that he's not involved with every pitch like, say, the pitcher and the catcher. Even the shortstop is a lot closer to the action so he relays signs to the outfield. It was a duty that Maury loved to do, especially when it came to positioning me out in left.

"Tommy was in his usual daze out there in the outfield and wasn't looking in the dugout for signs between pitches," Maury told a reporter. "So I look back and move him with my hand. Well, Tommy doesn't like me telling him what to do so he just cocks his head and puts his hands on his hips, and he doesn't move. A pitch later, I do the same thing and try to position him with my hand. He does the same thing, cocks his head and hands on his hips. We were arguing without yelling."

Once we got back to the dugout, Maury tried to act tough and called me out and started riding me. I'd had it with him so I went after him in the dugout. I had five guys holding me back. So of course, knowing that five guys are holding me back, Maury feels tough so he's saying, "Let him go. Let him go." Today, though, Maury admits, "I don't know what I would have done had they let him come after me." The blowup happened in the heat of the 1966 pennant race, in early September at home against the San Francisco Giants. So tensions were high.

Power Naps

Lou Johnson was one of the all-time great characters in the Dodgers clubhouse, whether they were playing in Los Angeles or in Brooklyn. Lou had this routine where he would go to sleep for 30 seconds. He'd be carrying on and talking and then all of a sudden he would just close his eyes and go to sleep while he was talking. It was like he was narcoleptic. He was just completely out—even snoring. Then he'd wake up 30 seconds later and say something like, "I'm ready to go." Wide awake, ready to go.

I'd look at him and just think, "What is he doing?" But he would be ready to go. He said it was because he had to recapture his thought process with that power nap, a power burst.

"I could do that," Lou said. "If you rode as many buses as I had, you could too. You had to be able to re-charge those batteries at a moment's notice."

Lou supplied the Dodgers and their fans with a lot of electric moments in his short but just as sweet time with the Dodgers. Sweet Lou, as he was and is still known, signed with the Yankees as an amateur free agent in 1953. But it wasn't until 12 years later, in 1965, that he got his first real break. And that came courtesy of my big break—when I broke my ankle. Lou had spent most of his time in the minor leagues. Before the Dodgers called him up, Lou had only played in 96 major league games up to that point. That year, with the Dodgers, he played in 131 games and helped take us to the World Series.

A Happy Fella

A player is always excited when he hits a home run, but Lou was really happy when he went deep. As he rounded the bases, he would be smiling and clapping. And not just a regular clap; he was clapping non-stop, all the way around the bases and grinning that wide grin of his.

He liked to say, "I'm just happy to be here," and that was true. But a lot of the other teams, especially their pitchers, didn't take too kindly to his celebrations around the bases. Lou was hit by pitches 16 times that year, and remember, he didn't come up to the Dodgers until May. So that's a lot of bruises in a short amount of time. Lou held the Dodger team record for most times hit by a pitch in a single season with those 16 plunks until Alex Cora got hit 18 times in 2004. Lou says he was hit so much because he hung out over the plate when he was batting. In any event, five days after joining the Dodgers, Lou beat the Houston Colt .45s with a 10th-inning home run. He was celebrating that 3-2 win on that run around the bases like crazy. Three days later, Houston pitcher Bob Bruce hit Lou in the head with a fastball that crushed Lou's batting helmet, and Lou had to spend some time in the hospital.

Some of our own teammates didn't care for his clapping. They thought it showed up the other pitcher and, of course, that could mean another one of our guys would get hit by a pitch in retaliation for Lou's celebrations. Not that he cared.

"I wasn't listening to that shit," Lou said. "I was happy and I was producing."

It's true. In our late drive to the 1965 pennant, Lou was absolutely clutch. He beat the Giants in the 15th inning. He beat the Braves with an 11th-inning single. He singled to beat the Reds in the 12th inning. He had a 13-game hitting streak near the end of the season in which he batted .556 in the last four games of the run. He scored the game-winning run in the pennant-clinching game against the Milwaukee Braves on October 2 and it was Lou's solo home run in Game 7 of the World Series against the Minnesota Twins that proved to be the winning run.

"Johnson's the guy," Sandy Koufax said at the time. "If it had not been for the job he did, we might not be here today."

Lou even got a special citation at City Hall because of his heroics.

An Advance, Please

As soon as Lou Johnson was called up to the Dodgers, the first thing he wanted to do was buy a house in L.A. That way he could really feel like he was a part of the team and the city. After so many years of riding buses in small minor league towns, he could truly feel as though he made it to the big city. He was going to buy John Roseboro's old house in Compton, but Lou didn't have the money in hand yet. So he went to Buzzie Bavasi and he asked for a loan— an advance. That didn't work. Buzzie couldn't believe his ears and in as few words as possible, he told Lou to get out of his office.

But Lou always thought that Buzzie had a soft spot in his heart for him. After hitting that game-winning homer against Houston in his first start with the Dodgers on May 10, 1965, Lou looked up to the press box on his way back to the dugout and tipped his cap to Buzzie. Lou thought Buzzie had pulled some strings to get him in the starting lineup. Buzzie was furious. But so was Houston, and the Colt .45s would get Lou a couple of days later. Buzzie told him to not do that again. Ever.

Shooting Stick with the Devil

They used to call Jim Gilliam "The Devil." It wasn't because he was evil or anything. Far from it. It was because of his pool playing ability. He was a great pool player. Both he and Walter Alston could play some pool. But with Jim, we'd go into these little towns during spring training and he'd go into the pool halls and issue a challenge, "Who wants the Devil? Who wants the Devil?" He didn't even carry his own stick. He didn't need it. He could play with anything. And he could play any game, eight-ball, nine-ball, whatever.

Good Eye, Bad Eye

Each year, it seemed like Jim Gilliam would walk 95 to 100 times. He had a great eye. And it was established how good his eye was at the plate. He still holds the Dodger rookie record with the 100 walks he had in 1953, and the 1,036 walks he had in his career are second in franchise history, behind Pee Wee Reese's 1,210. Jim had such a good eye that in 1961 he struck out only 34 times in 531 plate appearances. For his career, he struck out only once for every 20 plate appearances.

But we'd be driving down the street in spring training, and he'd drive right through a stop sign and I'd say, "Jim, what's wrong with you?" He'd say, "Oh, I didn't see that." Incredible. In a 14-year career, he averaged 74 walks because of how good his eye was, and yet he'd still drive right through a stop sign. Jim was actually the first Dodger to hit a home run at Dodger Stadium, taking the Cincinnati Reds' Moe Drabowski deep in the third inning of our 6-2 defeat of the Reds on April 11, 1962.

Ron Fairly thought of Jim as an inspiration, too.

"Jim Gilliam might have been the best ballplayer I ever played with," Ron said. "And I played with some guys that were damn good. He never missed a sign. He was a card player who had card sense, was street-wise and had a great feeling. He was the best second baseman I played next to. Jim would move on the infield with certain pitchers on the mound and it was unbelievable how good he was at having a feel for the game. He used to let me know a lot of times when a left-handed hitter was up that an off-speed pitch was coming because just before the pitch was coming he'd simply say, 'Ronnie.' I could hear it, which meant here comes an off-speed pitch. I could hear it just as a pitcher was getting ready to deliver the ball so the hitter couldn't hear it, but I could hear it and know it's coming. When Jim would move one way or the other, I would move with him. So if he went closer toward second base I went toward him and I'd move off the bag a little bit. Or if he moved closer toward the line then I'd move closer to the line as well.

"One time Eddie Mathews was hitting, and Jim moved over in the hole toward me and I started to move and he said, 'No, you stay there.' I'll be darned if two pitches later Eddie Mathews hit a line drive at me that hit me in the wrist, ricocheted right to Gilliam and he threw the ball to first and they got him. Jimmy was right there.

"All Jimmy could do was beat you. He did nothing fancy. He'd walk. He'd steal a base, he'd get a base hit late in the ballgame, and that's one of the reasons why we were a good ball club."

Jim was at his best against the best. During our 1963 World Series championship season, Jim batted .311 against the St. Louis Cardinals and .319 against the San Francisco Giants and scored the winning runs in each of the last three games of the World Series against the New York Yankees. He was clutch and he came out of retirement as a member of Alston's staff to help us win the World Series in 1965. He should have been a manager. He managed in the Puerto Rican winter league and did really well, and he was on Tommy Lasorda's staff as his hitting coach until he died of a cerebral hemorrhage two days before the start of the 1978 World Series. He was only 49 years old, nine days shy of his 50th birthday. The Dodgers honored him by wearing a Number 19 patch on the left arm of their uniforms during the Fall Classic. I've said it before and I'll say it again: Jim should be in the Hall of Fame.

I'm Going to Miss Him

The so-called Bonus Baby rule, which stipulated that if you signed for at least $4,000 then you had to spend your first two years on the major league roster, affected a lot of players in a negative way early in their career. Perhaps none were more affected than Willie Crawford. It hurt his development. Willie was signed for $100,000 out of Fremont High School in Los Angeles two days after graduation in 1964 by Tommy Lasorda. Then Willie found himself riding the bench of the defending World Series champions. He was only 17 years old and his signing bonus was the second highest paid by the Dodgers at the time (only Frank Howard had received more). But there were a lot of good ballplayers on our team, and Willie Crawford couldn't break into the lineup.

From 1964 through 1967, Willie played in only 72 games and batted .210 with no home runs and no RBIs. I talked to him early on about keeping his spirits up. I told him that anything was possible—he could get traded to another organization and get a shot, get some at-bats. But no matter what, when you go out there on the field, always do the best that you can, because you never know who's looking at you. Once he did get in, he showed he could play. He could have been an everyday ballplayer for a different team when he first came up. In fact, he got a pinch-hit single in Game 1 of the 1965 World Series against the Minnesota Twins. Willie could run, he could hit, he could field. His arm was pretty good. He just couldn't break in. But when he did finally break in and get a lot of at-bats as a regular, he batted .295, twice. Willie even hit a home run for the Dodgers in the 1974 World Series against the Oakland A's.

Having never played in the minor league definitely hurt him and his development. He should have played one year in the minors—that would have been key for him. He could fly. He was a great athlete in high school. He was a quarterback in football, ran track, competed in the long jump, and was All-City in baseball and football. Lasorda once said that Willie could have been a great college football player. Easily. Who was going to catch him? He should have played more earlier in his career. Willie died late in the summer of 2004 of kidney disease. He was only 57 years old. I'm going to miss him.

Leo the Lip Comes Aboard

We had an unusual situation on the coaching staff in 1961. That's when Leo "The Lip" Durocher was hired by Mr. O'Malley to be the third-base coach on Walt Alston's staff. It was unusual because Durocher was his own person. He had already managed the Brooklyn Dodgers from 1939 through 1948—winning the 1941 pennant—and our hated rivals, the New York Giants, from 1948 until 1955. In Harlem, he won two pennants for the Giants, in 1951 and 1954 and won the 1954 World Series.

Durocher spoke his mind. Remember, he's the guy who coined the phrase "nice guys finish last" and made it so popular. He was a great manager, even though he got in trouble. He was strictly a ballplayer's coach. One time he got mad at Frank Howard and he went after him. Durocher wasn't that big of a guy, maybe five foot 10, 160 pounds. And Frank is a monster at 6-7, 255. But Durocher went after him. Frank was sitting down and just looked up, "Are you mad at me? You're not mad at me, are you?" He said it with such a calm and sarcastic tone that Durocher just went nuts. We all had to hold him back because he was going crazy.

Durocher knew all the gangsters at the time so you didn't mess with him. He talked about being one of those guys who put cherry bombs in the pockets of new suits and laughed when they exploded. He was a shortstop who had played with St. Louis Cardinals' Gashouse Gang as well as with the New York Yankees, Cincinnati Reds and Dodgers. He was Old School before Old School became hip.

Leo Durocher (left) was a unique individual and a Dodger through and through. He rubbed elbows with the likes of Jackie Robinson (right) and nearly traded blows with guys like Moose Skowron and Frank Howard. Courtesy of the Los Angeles Dodgers

While Alston was real quiet, Durocher was a little flamboyant. He had a lot of stories to tell and he commanded a lot of attention. He knew everybody. If Alston had to let him know that he was the man, he would do that. I tried to stay out of the drama. I was young and stuff like that didn't affect me. But I think it affected the rest of the team. I was in hog heaven, so I didn't pay much mind to Durocher doing things behind Alston's back.

Moose Skowron said he had a confrontation with Durocher that ended in a figurative handshake rather than in throwing fists.

"Leo was trying to get Walt Alston's job," Moose said. "I got real angry at that. I lost all respect for Leo after that. One time he told me to take out the opposing second baseman, and I told him that wasn't my job, I don't do that. I ripped Leo's ass and I told him that he was the worst coach I had ever seen. And we became very good friends after that, all because I ripped his ass.

"But Frank Howard and Leo didn't get along at all. I heard he put Leo up on a hanger one time."

It's true, Durocher definitely rubbed Frank the wrong way. Especially because Frank didn't care for the way Durocher hazed rookies. Durocher seemed to take a perverse glee in messing with pitcher Joe Moeller when he first came up and, according to Ron Fairly, Frank told Durocher, "Leave the kid alone or I'll knock you on your fucking ass." Durocher never messed with the kid again. I guess Durocher learned his lesson.

He coached on Alston's staff from 1961 until 1964.

The Voice of the Dodgers

Vin Scully has been known as the Voice of the Dodgers since 1950, when they still played in Brooklyn. He's been around long enough, though, that he's also the eyes and ears of the Dodgers. He's probably seen and felt more heartache and joy than anyone associated with the organization still living. And he still gets surprised by the game to this day.

"When I started, my first year in 1950, we lost the pennant on the last day of the season on a wrong-field home run," Vin reminded me, and as a Dodger fan back then, I didn't want to remember. "Dick Sisler, a left-handed batter, hit a home run to left field and beat Don Newcombe. I thought, in 1950, 'Whoa, I'll never have to go through anything like that again.' Then in 1951 we had this big lead, 13 1/2 games in August, and when it's all over, we lose on the home run by Bobby Thomson and I thought, 'Okay, I'll never ever have to see anything like that again.' And then, of course, 1962 brought it all back again."

Ah yes, 1962. Don't remind me.

Tommy Trojan in Right Field

After Frank Howard was traded to the Washington Senators in the winter of 1964, Ron Fairly essentially took over right field. Ron also played a lot of first base. Longtime famed Los Angeles broadcaster Stu Nahan remembers Ron wearing his college alma mater loyalties on his sleeve.

"Fairly was a Trojan, and he never forgot the fact that he was a USC Trojan," Stu said. "All Fairly was worried about was if USC won or lost. If they lost, it was like the end of the world was in sight. He and his wife would go to every USC function. Fairly was Tommy Trojan."

Ron didn't dispute it: "Oh yeah. I'm a big Trojan fan to this day. Growing up in Southern California, why not?"

Like a Fire Hydrant

I always felt like catcher John Roseboro had my back, no matter what. Even if I always felt that he was a little bit angry about something. And I was always glad that I had him as a teammate. He was a leader but he was far from a cheerleader. He led by example and was looked up to by just about everyone on the team. He had a funny nickname as well that belied his personality.

"We called him 'Gabby' because he didn't say anything," Ron Fairly said with a laugh. "But when he did have something to say, you shut up and you listened. He had such a great feel for working with the pitcher. And he was so good at blocking the plate. If he thought you were going to run over him, he'd hurt you. It was kind of like sliding into a fire hydrant. The fire hydrant doesn't give much. But if you just came in and slid, you were fine. He'd tag you out and roll around and hold onto the ball and everything was fine. One guy tried to run over him and he flipped him. About 20 minutes later, they woke him up and moved him."

I was just glad I never tried to run Gabby over when I left the Dodgers. In fact, my first year away from the Dodgers he helped me out when I was trying to bat .300. And he wasn't your stereotypical catcher. John could run . . . for a catcher. From 1958 through 1963, he led all major league catchers in steals, six straight years. And in 1961, he grounded into just one double play the entire season, in 394 at-bats. Catching takes its toll, though, and in 1964 he was in the whirlpool so much that we renamed it the USS Roseboro.

The Man of a Thousand Stances

Willie Davis picked up a nickname because of his ability to imitate other players when they were at bat. They called him "The Man of a Thousand Stances." It depended upon whatever town we were playing in. We'd play in Pittsburgh and all of a sudden Willie's up at the plate batting like Roberto Clemente. We'd go to Milwaukee or Atlanta and Willie's turned into Hank Aaron. In San Francisco, he's Willie Mays. I told him to just be himself. The funny thing about it was that Willie Davis had success in just about every stance he batted in, especially down the stretch of the 1963 season. On the way to the World Series, Willie batted .313 in September and .426 in the final 13 games.

"I finally found a stance that felt right," Willie said at the time, "and I'll start that way in 1964."

Willie Davis used to crack us up because he never had a batting stance of his own—he'd copy everyone else's style—even though he had great success at the plate and set many L.A. Dodger franchise records that still stand today. Courtesy of the Los Angeles Dodgers

By the time his career with the Dodgers came to an end after the 1973 season, when the Dodgers traded him to the Montreal Expos for relief pitcher Mike Marshall, Willie had set Los Angeles Dodgers records for hits (2,091), extra-base hits (585), triples (110), at-bats (7,495), runs (1,004) and total bases (3,094). Besides that, he had a 31-game hitting streak in 1969 that still stands as the franchise record, and he led the National League with a club-record 16 triples in 1970.

I always told him to just be himself and he had his own stance, and it was a proud one, when he came back to Dodger Stadium with the Expos in 1974 and got five hits to help Montreal beat the Dodgers, 8-7. That was a good payback for The Man of a Thousand Stances.

A Different Kind of One-Hitter

When Roy Gleason was coming up through the minor leagues, he was seen as a heavy hitter and big swinger who struck out too much. I remember him as a guy who was always getting into trouble with his group of buddies. I know they messed up the infield somewhere, I think it was in the Instructional League. They went and put water all over the infield at night and flooded it.

Roy was a good prospect who was from Los Angeles and, as a high school pitcher at Garden Grove High School, he had an earned-run average of 0.93. He would sometimes throw batting practice to the Dodgers at the Coliseum. He had some speed as an outfielder, but his major league career lasted all of one official at-bat in eight games. He was a late-season call up in 1963 and he was used seven times as a pinch runner. He thought that the only guy on the team faster than him was Willie Davis. In his lone at-bat, Roy pinch hit for relief pitcher Phil Ortega on September 28 against the Philadelphia Phillies. Facing Dennis Bennett, Roy drove an inside fastball down the left-field line for a double.

"I thought I was going to be a superstar," Roy told the *Los Angeles Times* 40 years after his lone big-league hit.

But with the Dodger outfield loaded, Roy ended up returning to the minor leagues before being drafted by the Army in 1967 and being sent to Vietnam, where he was a point man on some missions in the jungle. He was injured there when a shell exploded in a tree above him and his left calf and left wrist were seriously wounded. He tried to make a comeback in baseball, but he was later involved in a car accident and his career was finished.

Still, he became the only player with previous major league experience to serve in Vietnam, and he also became the only Dodger to receive a Purple Heart. He also earned a Bronze Star and 14 overall military citations. And his lifetime batting average is still a perfect 1.000.

5

REDEMPTION IN THE
1963 WORLD SERIES

A Dream Match Up

Hollywood could not have written a better script for the 1963
World Series. In one corner was the establishment, the New York
Yankees. They were already appearing in their 28th Fall Classic and
they were heavy favorites, having gone 104-57 for their manager,
Ralph Houk, and winning the American League pennant by 10 1/2
games over the Chicago White Sox. And they did it with Mickey
Mantle and Roger Maris injured most of the year. Mickey played in
only 52 games and still hit 15 home runs and Roger, who had set the
single-season home run record with 61 homers two years earlier,
played in just 86 games but still went deep 23 times. Still, the Bronx
Bombers hit 188 home runs as a team and Elston Howard was the
AL's Most Valuable Player after hitting 28 homers. In the other corner sat us, the Dodgers, the same team that had left Brooklyn for the
West Coast five years earlier. We only hit 110 home runs as a team
that year and Frank Howard was the only one on the team to hit
more than 20, with 28 homers and 64 RBIs. I helped out by win-

ning my second straight National League batting title with a .326 average, 16 homers and 88 RBIs. Maury Wills batted .302 and stole 40 bases while Ron Fairly hit 17 homers and Jim Gilliam batted .282. We went 99-63 and had to hold off a late charge by the St. Louis Cardinals to win the NL flag even though we lost three straight to end the season. We could hardly wait to get the World Series started. It was truly a homecoming for me, and Sandy, a couple of Brooklyn boys. The Dodgers had won their first World Series in 1955 against the Yankees in a Subway Series, and while it was sweet to beat the Yankees for that championship, a lot of Dodger fans still wanted a lot more payback, especially for the six previous World Series defeats at the hands of the Bronx Bombers.

Bill "Moose" Skowron provided an extra subplot. He had reluctantly come to the Dodgers in a trade with the Yankees the previous November. Now he had a shot at a little payback himself.

"It was tough, but things happen," Moose said of the business end of baseball. "They traded me for Stan Williams, and the Yankees gave me a big raise before I left so that was good. But I didn't produce with the Dodgers in the regular season. I had a rough time with the National League pitchers. When a hitter and pitcher are seeing each other for the first time, the advantage always goes to the pitcher. I was lousy.

"It started in spring training when I got jammed by both Sandy Koufax and Don Drysdale in batting practice and my thumb just puffed up. Then, early in the season in Chicago, it was a cold day, and I got jammed again and it puffed up again. I was overmatched.

"But that Dodger team was one of the greatest teams I ever played with. With all that pitching and hitting, it was amazing. Everybody had a great year except me. What surprised me was that Ron Fairly had a good year and then Mr. Alston told me that I was playing first base. I was lousy. I struggled all season long. I ended up batting .203 but I was playing in the World Series. I still don't know why."

For many reasons, the 1963 World Series was sweeter than candy because of how we beat the Yankees—in four straight games—giving L.A. its second world championship in four years.

"When we got to the World Series, it really didn't matter who was coming in from the American League," Maury told the Dodgers more than 40 years later when the club was celebrating an anniversary of the series. "We were just excited to get there and play for the trophy. But when it was the Yankees, that made it all the more special because of the mystique of the New York Yankees, of playing in Yankee Stadium."

And that's where we went for Game 1.

Sandy Deals in Game 1

On October 2, 1963, you could cut the tension at Yankee Stadium with a knife. Hall of Famers Joe Dimaggio and Stan Musial were at the game, and Musial threw out the ceremonial first ball from the stands, where 69,000 fans sat.

Two future Hall of Fame lefties were also the starting pitchers for Game 1. Sandy Koufax, who led the National League with 25 wins and a record 306 strikeouts while winning the first of his three Cy Young Awards, was on the hill for us. He later said that taking the mound at Yankee Stadium, which was so huge, was like looking up from the bottom of the Grand Canyon. Whitey Ford, who had won a World Series-record 10 games, was throwing for the Yankees. Whitey would throw a mud ball. He would throw a pitch, and the Yankee catcher, Elston Howard, would get the ball and quickly rub it in the ground and throw it back with the dirt caked on it. That would off-center the ball, and Whitey didn't know where the ball was going to go. He'd throw it and it would just take off. And if the dirt was a little wet? Oh my God. That was a mud ball. But we were able to get to him that day.

The bigger the stage, the better Sandy Koufax pitched. He was at the top of his game against the Yankees in the Bronx during Game 1 of the 1963 World Series, silencing the Bombers with a record 15 Ks. Courtesy of the Los Angeles Dodgers

It was Sandy who was next to un-hittable, striking out the first five batters he faced on the way to setting a new strikeout record for a World Series game with 15 Ks that day. That beat the previous record of 14 set by the Brooklyn Dodgers' Carl Erskine in Game 3 of the 1953 World Series, also against the Yankees. The record came 10 years to the day after Erskine set the mark, when he struck out Mickey Mantle four times. Sandy got Mickey twice. After he struck out the first time, Mickey looked back at Johnny Roseboro and said, "How in the fuck are you supposed to hit that stuff?" At least that's what Johnny said that Mickey told him.

Sandy's curveball was nastier than his fastball. It would start way up here, head high, and then Roseboro would catch it just above the plate and the umpire would call it low. So I'm in the outfield, wondering, "If he called it low and it started way up here, what happened in between there? It had to cross the plate." Koufax was on that day.

Putting It Away

But even with Sandy on, we still had to manufacture at least one run to win the opening game. We got five to win, 5-2. As it turned out, Roseboro got all we would need with a three-run homer in the second inning. There was also some vindication for Moose. He made the Yankees pay when he singled home a run in the second inning and drove in another run in the third, giving us an insurmountable 5-0 lead.

The Yankees didn't get on the scoreboard until the eighth inning, when Tom Tresh went deep for a two-run homer. Sandy settled down, though, and he set the strikeout record when he got pinch hitter Harry Bright for the final out. The Yankees only got six hits on the day and after the game, Sandy needed all five fingers on Roseboro's hand, in addition to his own 10 digits, to represent all of his strikeouts. Sandy's World Series strikeout record stood for five years, until the St. Louis Cardinals' Bob Gibson struck out 17 Detroit Tigers in 1968.

Hey, Herman!

Coming back to play at Yankee Stadium was definitely a special experience for me. I had a lot of family and friends come to those first two games. I was in the outfield concentrating, locked into the game. It was the World Series, after all. But then I heard, "Tommy!

Tommy!" just getting louder each and every time. Then they yelled, "Hey, Herman!" That's my given name. So I was like, "Oh shit, somebody knows me." So I turned around between pitches, "Hey, what's up?"

Speaking Softly

Mrs. O'Malley had a soft voice. She had cancer of the larynx and had an opening in her throat, a tracheotomy, so she would speak really softly. So before Game 2, me and Willie Davis went over to pay our respects and say hello to her. We were excited. But when we got there, Willie starts whispering to her, "How are you, Mrs. O'Malley?" He was talking real soft, as if it were her ears that were sensitive. We walked away and I said, "Willie, what are you doing?" He talked like that right back to her. It just rolled off her back. That was just nervousness on Willie's part.

Podres Wins Game 2

Johnny Podres, who beat the Yankees twice in the magical 1955 World Series, including a 2-0 complete-game shutout in Game 7 at Yankee Stadium, started Game 2 for us. The Yankees countered with left-hander Al Downing, who would come to the Dodgers in 1971 and would give up Hank Aaron's historic 715th home run on April 8, 1974 in Atlanta.

But on this day, Johnny would have to reach deep to beat the Yankees again. Years later, Johnny recounted his thrilling victory for the Dodgers when the club revisited the 1963 World Series.

"I remember my final start of the season against Philadelphia, it was a tune-up for the World Series, and I gave up eight runs in 1 2/3 innings," Johnny said. "But Alston told Drysdale that he had to have a lefty pitch at Yankee Stadium, so I got the start and I had a great game."

Johnny always seemed to step up in the clutch. Besides beating the Yankees twice in 1955, he also won Game 2 of the 1959 World Series against the Chicago White Sox. Against the Yankees that day, he held them to one run on six hits and a walk with four strikeouts in 8 1/3 innings and we won, 4-1, to take a 2-0 lead in the series heading home.

Willie got us out to a quick lead with a two-run double in the first inning and Moose went deep for a solo shot in the fourth. Johnny was going for a complete game when Alston pulled him in the ninth inning.

"I've got the Yankees shut out 4-0 and Hector Lopez hit a slow curve off me for a double," Johnny said. "Alston came running out and said, 'Are you okay, John?' I said, 'Yeah Skip, I'm all right, I feel good.' He said, 'You sure you're all right? I've got Perry ready.'"

He was talking about reliever Ron Perranoski.

"Alston asked me again if I was all right and about the third time he asked me, I said, 'Walt, are you trying to tell me that you want to bring Perry in the game?' He said, 'Yeah.' So I said, 'What are you waiting for? Bring him in.'"

Perry was our bullpen leader that year, going 16-3 with 21 saves and a 1.67 ERA in 69 appearances. He wasn't quite lights-out against the Yankees that day, though, giving up a single to Elston Howard that scored Lopez. But he got the final two outs and struck out Clete Boyer to end it as we headed west, to home.

"I'm really glad that he brought Perry in, because as it turned out, he was our only reliever to pitch in the series," Johnny said. "It was great that he got the chance. As long as we won the series, that was fine with me." It was fine with all of us.

Getting Rid of Maris

The best thing I did in the World Series that year was get rid of Roger Maris. That may sound kind of harsh, but it's true. I didn't do anything out of the ordinary to do it, either. All I did was hit a pop fly down the right field line in the third inning of Game 2. While Maris chased my ball down in the right-field corner, he ran into the iron railing down there, injuring his knee and elbow. He would not play in the series again. My blooper ended up a triple, but it looked like a line drive in the scorebook—so I'll take it. I hit another triple in the eighth inning and became one of six players in World Series history to get two triples in a single game.

Looking Back

As special as opening the 1963 World Series in New York was, it was not the first time I had played a game at Yankee Stadium. True, I had my own locker at The House the Ruth Built when I worked out there in high school, but as a Dodger, we actually played an exhibition game there once. They called it The Sandlot Games because it raised money for the sandlots in New York.

I didn't start the game, but I got into it in the middle and I got a base hit. I thought I was Jackie Robinson so I stole second. I was just having fun so I took a pretty good lead off second base. I was jumping around, back and forth. Tony Kubek, the Yankees short-stop, ran around behind me so I headed back toward second. But as I was watching Kubek go back to his position, Bobby Richardson, the second baseman, came back around to the bag. Bang! I didn't even know it. They threw the ball to second before I could even move. I said, "Bobby, if you can, let me be safe because I've got a whole bunch of my friends out here. Please let me get back here safe-ly. Do something where I can get back." I had purchased 40 tickets for friends and family to come to the game. He said, "I'm sorry, Tommy, I've got to tag you out." I was embarrassed. So were my 40 friends and family.

Come Together

That plane ride back home after our win in Game 2 was full of quiet confidence. A lot of guys played cards or gambled to pass the time. We were up 2-0 and we were just thinking one game at a time. We were playing as a team and everybody was having some success. That's a good feeling—to have everyone clicking together like that. It was a great feeling to see Roseboro hit a home run in Game 1 because I always felt like he had my back. I knew he was there for me if I needed him. We were neighbors. We lived in Compton, along with Charlie Neal, before Charlie was sent to the New York Mets in the winter of 1961. Roseboro and I were always good friends. He catered to Maury Wills as much as I catered to Willie Davis. The younger set and the older set, coming together. That's how it felt in the 1963 World Series. We were just coming together as one and we just needed two more wins to close it out.

Big D Deals in Game 3

On October 5, 1963, Dodger Stadium, in just its second year of existence, played host to its first ever World Series game before a crowd of 55,912. When it opened, Dodger Stadium was called a pitcher's park. How appropriate it was, then, that Game 3 was another classic pitcher's duel with Don Drysdale, who won 19 games that year, going for us against Jim Bouton, who would later write a scathing and polarizing tell-all book, *Ball Four,* about what goes on behind closed doors in the major leagues. The Yankees were so upset with him for writing that book that they didn't invite him back to Yankee Stadium until 1998. I was his teammate in 1969 with the Seattle Pilots, and he included me in the book. Guys who didn't like the book but liked me referred to me as "Bouton's Bobo." They were joking, but I still didn't care for that. Bouton also was the founder of "Big League Chew," a chewing gum that came in a packet that resembled chewing tobacco. But in 1963, in only his second year in the majors, Bouton had won 21 games for the Yankees with an ERA of 2.53. It was no surprise that the final score of Game 3 was 1-0.

I was fortunate enough to produce the lone run of the game with a single in the first inning that scored Gilliam, who had walked on "ball four" and moved to second base on, ironically enough, a Bouton wild pitch. That one run was enough for Big D, who went the distance and allowed just three hits and a walk while striking out nine batters. Bouton was almost as good, going seven innings and allowing the one run on four hits and five walks. That was the way we played. Our feeling was that if we got one or two runs, with our pitching, we were in good shape with a great chance to win. That was often the case. If we got four or five runs, that was a bonus.

But the win did not come without drama. Clinging to our one-run lead, and with two outs in the ninth inning, Joe Pepitone drove a high fly ball to right field. I thought it had a shot at going out. Luckily for us, Ron Fairly caught it at the wall to end the game and put us one win away from the unimaginable—a four-game sweep of the Yankees.

"When he hit it, I thought it had a chance," Ron said later. "Then it got up there and died. At that point, I knew that game was over and it started to sink in just how special this series could be, because you don't beat the Yankees four straight."

The Yankees had beaten the Dodgers so much in their history. The opportunity to sweep them was sweet—simply unbelievable. And I had something to do with that—I hit .400, tops in the series.

Sandy Again, in Game 4

It was a glorious Sunday afternoon and we had a chance to win L.A.'s second World Series in five years. To do so on this day we would have to sweep the Yankees for just the second time in their then-28 World Series appearances. We had our best going for us in Sandy Koufax, and it was a rematch of Game 1 since Whitey Ford was pitching for the Yankees. Whitey was on his game this time. In seven innings he only gave up two hits. But they were big enough

So much pent-up frustration turned into a wild celebration and spilled onto the Dodger Stadium infield when we got the last out of the four-game sweep of the Yankees in the 1963 Fall Classic. The party was on. Courtesy of the Los Angeles Dodgers

hits to give us the 2-1 win and the World Series trophy. Sandy was named MVP of the series after pitching a complete-game six-hitter and not walking a batter while striking out eight Yankees. It was the greatest pitching performance that I had ever seen to that point.

Big Frank Draws First Blood

Frank Howard drew first blood in the fifth inning with a mammoth 430-foot shot to the Loge Level in left field. It was the first home run to land in the orange seats in Dodger Stadium's history and it is still one of only 13 to reach that level in 43 seasons.

In the seventh, Mickey Mantle came out of his series-long slumber with a game-tying solo blast to left-center. He hadn't been contributing all series so we knew he was going to break out of it sooner or later. He ended up batting .133 for the series, going two for 15. You've got to watch out with a guy like him.

The brooms began to surface in the bottom of the seventh. That's when Jim Gilliam led off the inning by hitting a high hopper to Clete Boyer at third base. Boyer's throw to Pepitone at first was on target, but Pepitone lost the ball in the white shirts of the daytime crowd and the ball bounced off his wrist far enough away that Gilliam made it all the way to third on a three-base error. Willie Davis was up next and he did his job, hitting a sacrifice fly to center that scored Gilliam for the go-ahead run. But what would a World Series title be without more drama?

With two outs in the ninth and a Yankee at first, Hector Lopez hit a grounder in the hole at short that Maury ran down. Maury turned and fired to Dick Tracewski at second base for the force out, and the umpire ruled Bobby Richardson out. I was already halfway in from left field, running in to celebrate, but the ball squirted out of Dick's glove. Not only was Richardson safe at second, but a base hit would now tie the game—and Elston Howard was coming to the plate. He was a dangerous hitter. I just kept saying, "Get the last out.

Come on, Sandy, strike him out." But Maury made a hell of a play. Elston hit the ball to the same hole at short and Maury gloved it and threw to Dick at second. Dick held on this time, and Lopez was out at second. The celebration was on. Oh, was it ever.

A Buzz Kill

The clubhouse celebration was crazy. Champagne and beer were flowing everywhere. Guys were jumping all over the place. It was wild. But the champagne hadn't even dried in the clubhouse yet, when a dose of reality smacked Ron Fairly right in the face. It was at the victory party afterwards that Fresco Thompson, the Dodgers' vice president and director of minor league operations, asked Ron to stand up and "speak on behalf of the players who probably wouldn't be here next year." Talk about a buzz kill.

A Fond Look Back

If you looked at just our offensive stats, it would be hard to see how we swept the mighty Yankees. In the four games, we used only 13 players and scored a total of just 12 runs on 25 hits. Obviously, we had to rely on our pitching. It was definitely our strength in the regular season, when our pitching staff set a Los Angeles Dodger record for most shutouts in a season with 24 games that ended in goose eggs for our opponents. The 1988 World Series champion Dodgers, led by Orel Hershiser, also had 24 shutouts.

But in the 1963 Fall Classic, Sandy had two complete games, Don had one and Johnny went into the ninth inning of his game. Ron Perranoski was the only other pitcher to get any time for us, and he went less than an inning. Our pitchers gave up a total of four runs and 22 hits, and the Bronx Bombers batted just .171 for the series.

"When you played in the World Series, you always wanted to beat the best, and we beat the best," Johnny said later when reliving the story for the Dodgers.

"It was always a thrill to beat the Yankees." Maury agreed, saying, "We had no clue that we could win four in a row. Our idea coming in was to show some character, grind it out and try to scratch out a run here or there. It turned out that we got our usual outstanding pitching and our normal style of winning."

And Moose? Did he gain any extra satisfaction in beating his old club, one that he had played with for nine years?

"Not really," he said many years later. "It was just another game. I got 11 grand as a bonus for winning instead of eight grand for losing."

They were all correct, of course, but there was something more. With Sandy being from Brooklyn, I knew he felt it too. I had a lot of gratification when we swept the New York Yankees. That was unheard of. Being a Brooklyn guy, it was a special feeling having watched the Dodgers play all those World Series against the Yankees and come up short all but that one time. It wasn't that the torch had been passed—we muscled it away from them. The Yankees represented the 1950s. We were the 1960s. Maybe Vin Scully summed it up best.

"The 1963 World Series was probably the sweetest of all for anybody with the Dodgers," Vin said. "Not only to beat the Yankees but to beat them four straight."

It almost made the pain of 1962 go away. Almost.

6

THE FORMULA

Manufacturing Runs

The big knock on the Dodgers of the early 1960s was that we couldn't score enough runs for our pitchers. After one of Sandy Koufax's no-hitters, Don Drysdale supposedly said, "That's great, but did he win?" In 1962, I led the league in RBIs with 153. I didn't consider myself much of a power threat, but I did hit 27 homers that year. That was my single-season high for my career. Still, 153 RBIs, that's a lot.

"For two years Tommy was the best hitter in baseball," Sandy Koufax told a reporter, and I'm still blushing from the compliment. "He just didn't get the recognition. He was a part of a team that had a lot of good parts to it. I don't know why Tommy wasn't recognized, but Don, Maury and I received more recognition than the other guys on the team. Maybe it was because it was for just such a short time that he was doing it. He just came and did his job. People forget how well he could run. He was a big man but he could really run.

With small, fast guys like Willie Davis (far right) batting in front of me, and gargantuan monsters like Frank Howard (far left) hitting behind me, I was able to collect RBIs in bunches, even though they're the ones being recognized by The Sporting News *in this photo.*
Courtesy of the Los Angeles Dodgers

He wasn't as fast as Willie, but who was? Tommy hit the ball where it was pitched. He'd just send something out there and you'd look up at the scoreboard and it said, 'RBI, T. Davis.'"

How did I get all those ribbies? Willie Davis, Jim Gilliam and Maury Wills all hit in front of me, and big Frank Howard hit behind me. Willie, Jim and Maury were so fast and were such good hitters they'd all get on base. And then I'd hit a little single over the second baseman's head, and get three ribbies. Oh, they were flying. And Big Frank protected me in the lineup with his mere presence. Normally, a hitter will get one good pitch to hit each at bat. But because of

Frank Howard hitting behind me, I got more than my share of good pitches. Opposing pitchers didn't want to pitch to Frank because they were thinking about their livelihood and their life, because if Frank hits a line drive through the box, the guy pitching is likely to never see his family again. So I used to get two pitches to hit because nobody ever wanted to walk me. I took advantage of that.

Almost Gone

We were going through a bad stretch in 1961 and Walter Alston was looking for an excuse. We weren't playing so well and we were in St. Louis, and Alston said to me, "I heard you were playing golf." Well, we weren't supposed to play golf. First I said I wasn't playing and then I asked him, "Why would you say that?" So he said, "Well, I found out you were playing." I said, "Well, there's a whole bunch of us playing golf." I stopped it there. I didn't say anything else because I didn't want to let my emotions get the best of me and end up giving up the other guys.

But he said, "Oh, you're getting smart?" He was going to call Buzzie to have me kicked off the team. But Pete Reiser helped me back into good graces. I was disturbed about that because it just came out of the blue. I did respect him, but I didn't know why he said that.

Vin Scully later told me that during the winter meetings Charlie Finley, the owner of the Kansas City Athletics, was interested in me. They were going to trade me to Kansas City. But I think Finley found out I had a bad back because I had to go in traction after the season. I was hitting .318 and I hurt my back, so the whole last month I didn't play and ended up with a .278 average. For two weeks I was in traction, that's how bad my back was. Finley thought I had a really bad back and then he called off the trade. The next two years I led the league in hitting. With the Dodgers.

Don Drysdale was the prototypical power pitcher and intimidator of the era. Big D was never afraid to throw a little chin music or drill a batter in the ribs if the situation called for it. Courtesy of the Los Angeles Dodgers

to be a little bit of a rivalry. Sandy threw a little harder and Drysdale had to be an intimidator and use the inside pitch more often. Sandy didn't have to intimidate. He just threw it by hitters.

But Drysdale was just as important as Sandy to the team because he still won 25 games and the Cy Young Award in 1962. Those 25 wins are still a Dodger record for a right-hander. He broke in with Brooklyn in 1956 when he was 19 years old, and he led the Dodgers with 17 wins in the 1959 championship year with an ERA of 3.45. He also struck out a league-high 242 batters. So I'd say he established himself first. But I'd love to have both of them right now.

Maury Wills once said that when it came to Sandy Koufax and Don Drysdale, there was a bias within the Dodger organization that tilted toward Drysdale. Drysdale was local. He was the first L.A. Dodger to win a Cy Young Award after leading the National League in wins, strikeouts and innings pitched in 1962. And he was not from Brooklyn, like Sandy. So, I could understand why a lot of L.A. people would gravitate toward Drysdale. When the Dodgers moved to L.A. from Brooklyn, it was a huge story of the local boy making good with a homecoming. He was more newsworthy, I guess, for that reason.

But when Sandy got on the mound, it was worldly then. The whole world knew. Of course, Drysdale was no slouch, either. He could hit, now, don't forget. He hit seven home runs in a season, twice, in 1958 and 1965. Drysdale was used as a pinch hitter. He could play. But he was always falling down. Every time he pitched, he always ended up on the ground. I don't know how he got there, but he was always on the ground. I guess it was because he dove at balls. He stayed dirty, which was great. He definitely wanted to win.

I never hit against Sandy, other than in the occasional batting practice. And I only hit against Drysdale a few times after I was traded. But truth be told, I didn't want to face either one of them.

Simply the Best

I read somewhere once where Bob Gibson said he and Juan Marichal might be rubbed a little wrong because people say Sandy Koufax was the best pitcher of the 1960s, even though Sandy didn't really hit a groove until 1961 and he retired after the 1966 season. I can understand Gibby feeling like that. After all, Marichal won 191 games in the decade, 27 more than Gibson, 33 more then Don Drysdale and 54 more than Sandy. But for those years, Sandy was the best. I mean, overwhelmingly. He was the first pitcher to repeat as a Cy Young Award winner, and he won three overall, in 1963, 1965 and 1966. And that was when they gave out just one award total, not one to each league. He threw four no-hitters, which was a record until Nolan Ryan got him, and Sandy was 97-27 in his last four years. Hall of Famer Willie "Pops" Stargell once said that hitting against Sandy was like trying to drink coffee with a fork. In Sandy's last year, he had a record of 27-9 with a 1.73 ERA.

It seemed like every time we went out there, Sandy was throwing a one-hitter, a two-hitter or a three-hitter. Sandy used to complain about a little kink here, or that he was a little sore. So on the days he was scheduled to pitch, we'd go up to Sandy in the clubhouse just to check on him and we'd ask him, "How you feel, baby?" He wouldn't even look at us and he'd start rubbing his arm or his shoulder and say in a painful manner, "I've got a knot right here." So we'd walk away and laugh to ourselves and say, "Well, that's a two-hitter." But if he said he was feeling good, it was just the opposite—he got whipped. He wouldn't last the first inning sometimes. But if he complained, we were like, "Oh, don't worry about nothing."

A lot of people talk about how swollen or how bruised Sandy's elbow and arm would get after he'd pitch. But I never saw Sandy's arm. It wasn't my thing. Unless I was hurt and in the trainer's room with him, I didn't want to see him hurt.

Sandy Steps Up

Sandy Koufax threw four no-hitters, including a perfect game. He set numerous strikeout records and won a pair of World Series MVP awards. But the most impressive game I ever saw him pitch was on the last day of the 1966 regular season. We had a double-header at Philadelphia, and all we had to do was win one of those games against the Phillies to clinch the pennant. But if we were swept, then the Giants would make up a game, and if they won that, then we would have had to play another playoff with the Giants. And we all know what happened against them in 1962.

As luck would have it, we lost the first game against the Phillies. Talk about pressure. Sandy was starting the nightcap at Connie Mack Stadium on just two-days' rest and he could throw only fastballs because his arm was hurting him so much and his back was giving him troubles, too. We had a 6-0 lead in the ninth inning before the Phillies started a rally. Richie Allen led off and got on because of an error before Harvey Kuenn, Tony Taylor and Bill White all singled. The next thing we knew, our lead was 6-2 and there was a runner on base with no outs. Alston paid a visit to the mound and told Sandy that if another batter got on base, he was going to the bullpen. Sandy settled down and struck out Bob Uecker before Bobby Wine grounded out to score another run and get the Phillies within three.

The top of the Phillies' hitting order was coming up and I was just thinking, "Strike him out, Sandy." And that's what he did. Sandy reached deep—deeper than I ever saw him reach before—and struck out Jackie Brandt, the Phillies' lead-off hitter, on three pitches to end the game and give us the pennant.

That game was his greatest ever because we had to win it and he had his problems. No one knew at the time that that would end up being the final regular-season game of his career. In his last season, Sandy's record was 27-6 and he struck out 313 batters. After the game, Sandy was quoted as saying, "Thank God it's over." We thought he was talking about the game. Little did we know he could have been talking about his career.

Chemistry 101

A lot of our success in the 1960s was due to the make-up of the team and the chemistry we had in the clubhouse. As Ron Fairly put it, "There was a closeness on our ball club. We had a mutual respect for everybody. We knew the strengths of players on our team and we knew where maybe they weren't so strong."

It's true—a man's got to know his limitations. Our batting average for the most part was not very good. But we could all hit well late in the ballgame. We were good situational hitters. Sandy Koufax said we were a close-knit team also.

"It was kind of exciting for all of us," Sandy said. "It was a very exciting ball club with guys who did things special. It was an interesting group of characters and we all got along, for the most part. You put 25 guys together for that long a time and you're going to get something. But we got along. It was special."

Philosophy 101

It always gives me a warm feeling when players today say that they look back upon my generation in reverence and say that we served as an inspiration. There's no doubt that the Dodgers are a team steeped in tradition and history. The truth is, we even looked back at the guys who came before us as sources of inspiration. Ron Fairly remembers a saying of Roy Campanella that we used as a clubhouse slogan. "After a win, Campy used to say, 'Fellas, the team that won today is the team that's going to win again tomorrow.' It was that kind of attitude that carried over from Brooklyn to L.A.," Ron said.

An Empty Cupboard

If it was easy for me to get all those RBIs in 1962 because of the speedy guys on base in front of me, it was just as frustrating for the guys batting behind me who often found the cupboard empty. Ron Fairly was almost like another lead-off hitter for a stretch.

"The one year Tommy drove in 153 runs, Tommy hit and then Frank Howard hit and he drove in 119 runs and they drove in all the runs before I even came to the plate," Ron said. "I had a stretch there for a while when I was hitting behind Tommy that it seemed like for about three weeks I didn't hit with anyone in scoring position because Tommy knocked them all in and Tommy's standing at first base. People wondered how come I wasn't driving in any runs, but unless I hit it out of the ballpark, I'm not going to drive in any runs."

But when Ron did get the chance to drive runners home, he did just that. Even with the bases relatively empty in 1962, Ron still had 71 RBIs. With runners on base in 1963, Ron batted a team-high .341. But when there was no one on base, Ron hit just .212. He was also dangerous later in the season. In 1961, Ron batted .350 after the All-Star break.

"What Tommy did in those back-to-back years was remarkable," Ron said.

I wouldn't have been able to do it without having guys on base in front of me.

Built on Pitching

Once the Dodgers moved to Dodger Stadium, we underwent a massive identity change. No longer a power-hitting team, we were a team built on pitching, speed and defense.

"We didn't score a lot of runs, but we didn't get shut out much," said Sandy Koufax. "We'd score two or three runs and we'd be in the game."

That was never more clear than in 1966, when the four-man rotation of Sandy, Don Drysdale, Claude Osteen and a rookie named Don Sutton started all but eight games that season. The 1966 Dodger team set an L.A. record for lowest staff ERA at 2.62 and established another mark for fewest walks issued in a season with 356 bases on balls.

In fact, only one other pitcher—Joe Moeller—made a start that season for the Dodgers. He started eight times after doubleheaders. The next team to accomplish something similar was the Seattle Mariners in 2003, when their five-man rotation of Freddy Garcia, Jamie Moyer, Joel Pineiro, Ryan Franklin and Gil Meche started every game for them during the season. Ron Fairly had a good view of that accomplishment as the radio announcer for the Mariners. He also had a unique perspective.

"Three of the four members of that Dodger pitching staff are in the Hall of Fame," Ron said, referring to Koufax, Drysdale and Sutton. "Osteen, not in the Hall of Fame, has 40 career shutouts. Now what kind of stuff do you think you have to have to throw 40 career shutouts? How many pitchers today have 40 career shutouts? Osteen had a lot better stuff than what people thought he had. That's the staff you had to hit off every day."

We had a pitching staff for the ages. Too bad we didn't win the World Series that year.

Don't Forget About the D

Of course people knew the Dodgers for our pitching and speed. But we were also a good defensive team—expect for the left fielder, me.

"People didn't realize how good of a defensive team we were, with Willie Davis in center field who could run down anybody," Ron Fairly said. "We had a hell of a defensive club. We all make errors, but it was the plays we made that other people didn't make."

It's true. We synchronized things with our pitching, our speed, and defense. Hitting, though, was last, even behind the defense.

"Bam" in the Glove

The mere sight of Sandy Koufax on a pitcher's mound, even if it was in the bullpen, was enough to intimidate any batter . . . or make his own pitcher start to look over his shoulder. That happened on one hot and muggy day in Chicago. Because of the four-man rotation we used at the time, Sandy was scheduled to throw on the side in the bullpen that day as part of his workout regimen. But, according to Ron Fairly, Walt Alston had a talk with Sandy before the game and asked him if he could get an inning of work out of him if Johnny Podres, who was starting, got in trouble. Sandy was agreeable.

"So Johnny's pitching, and in the seventh inning he's struggling like mad," Ron said. "In the eighth inning he's struggling again and there's not a dry spot on his uniform. Sandy is warming up in the bullpen and you could hear down in that right field area Sandy popping that glove, 'Bam,' with that fastball. 'Bam.' And Johnny could hear it. Johnny gets into a jam and Walt comes out and he says to Johnny, 'How do you feel?' He said, 'I feel fine, Walt, how are you?' All the while you can hear this 'Bam' down in the right field corner. Alston looked at Johnny and Johnny asked Walt, 'Who do you have warming up?' as if Johnny didn't know, listening to that 'Bam' of a 100-mph fastball hitting the glove down there. Walt said, 'I've got Koufax warming up down there, what do you think?' Johnny said, 'He's the best pitcher in baseball. Why didn't you bring him in here the last inning? I was done in the seventh inning. Bring him in here and get me out of here.'

"Sure enough, Sandy came in and the game was over."

The bullpen catcher's glove wasn't the only one going "bam" after all.

The Replacement: A Hobo

When I went down with my injury, the Dodgers didn't have to look far to find a capable and exciting replacement. As Vin Scully put it, "When Tommy Davis broke his ankle in May of the 1965 season, the feeling was one of 'Well, there goes the pennant. There's no chance without Tommy Davis.' And here comes Lou Johnson."

Ron Fairly agreed, saying, "That opened the door for Lou, and Lou did a fabulous job when he came up with our ball club. He gave us a spark and he gave us an attitude that you still see in Lou Johnson today. He'd hit a ground ball down to third and he'd think it was a double because he wasn't going to stop at first base, he was going to keep on going. That was the attitude that Lou brought to our ball club."

Sandy Koufax remembers someone else being pegged as my immediate replacement.

"Tommy got hurt then Al Ferrara got hurt and then Lou came in," Sandy said. "He was funny. He was a breath of fresh air and we won. We might have won more easily with Tommy, but we still won, so that was good."

Wes Parker said that the players all went to Buzzie to get his take on things. "I thought the season was over when Tommy went down," Wes told a reporter. "We asked Buzzie, 'Who are you going to get to replace Tommy?' Buzzie said that every team out there wanted either Drysdale or Koufax in trade."

The Dodgers only had to look to the minor league team in Spokane, Washington. That's where Lou, who had been toiling in the minors for 13 years with six different organizations, was waiting to make like Maury Wills did in 1959 and become the Dodgers' catalyst. Except Lou almost didn't make it to join the Dodgers. The morning after I was injured, Peter O'Malley called Lou and told him, "We're sending you to Cincinnati." Well, that's all Lou heard, that the Dodgers were sending him to the Reds. He thought he'd been traded to the Reds. So he started going off on Peter on the phone, telling him, "Naw, Peter, I ain't going to no Cincinnati. They're just going to send me to the minor leagues and I've been down there too long. I ain't going. I'll retire first. I'm tired of this shit." So he hung up the phone. Lou yelled at Peter, the son of the owner, and then just hung up the phone.

A couple of minutes later, Peter called Lou back and asked, "Now, Lou, what was that about?" After Peter told him that I had been injured and that he was being promoted to replace me in the lineup, Lou was embarrassed but just as excited. He could only say, "Oh. Okay. Thanks." Lou said he was at the airport before he even hung up and got on the next plane to Cincinnati to join the Dodgers. And how was he greeted? Here's how the Dodger yearbook heralded his arrival: "The hobo of the minors quickly became a leader and filled the void caused by Davis' absence."

Hobo? Those were certainly different times.

The 1965 World Series

We were on such a high after clinching the National League pennant that Buzzie Bavasi said we could beat the Minnesota Twins in four straight in the World Series, which was a strange claim, because the Twins had such stars as Tony Oliva, Harmon Killebrew, Bobby Allison and Jim Kaat and they had won 102 games and won the American League by seven games over the Chicago White Sox. It actually took us seven games to win it. But, what most remember about that World Series, though, was Sandy Koufax skipping his Game 1 start to honor Yom Kippur, the holiest day on the Jewish calendar. Thousands, if not millions, of Jewish people across the country and world were inspired by Sandy's observance.

On an ESPN special, Sandy said, "It was no hard decision for me. It was just a thing of respect. I wasn't trying to make a statement, and I had no idea it would impact that many people."

After the Twins chased Don Drysdale and beat us in Game 1, 8-2, in Minneapolis, Don told Alston, "I bet you wish I was Jewish, too." The Twins also jumped on Sandy in Game 2, beating us, 5-1, and all of a sudden they had a two-game lead on us. Thankfully, we came home for three games and Dodger Stadium was good to us.

In Game 3, Claude Osteen got us back in the series by shutting out the Twins, 4-0, before Don evened things up with a 7-2 win. Lou Johnson and Wes Parker both hit home runs and we were on our way. Sandy was his usual brilliant self in Game 5, shutting out the Twins, 7-0, and we were one win away from our second World Series championship in three years and our third in seven.

But the Twins wouldn't die. They beat Osteen, 5-1, setting up another dramatic Game 7. Even though it was Don's turn in the rotation, Alston went with Sandy . . . on two days' rest. The Twins countered with Jim Kaat, who was also going on two-day's rest. Lou got us on the board first with his solo home run off the left-field foul pole in the second inning. Then Ron Fairly doubled and Wes Parker singled him home. That was all Sandy needed, even though all he had from the fifth inning on was his fastball. He threw a three-hitter.

Johnny Roseboro said that he asked Sandy in the fifth what was up with his curveball and Sandy said he just didn't have it. Johnny said, "Well, what the fuck are we going to do?" And according to Johnny, Sandy's answer was, "Fuck it, blow them away." That's exactly what Sandy did.

The Joint Holdout

We entered the 1966 season with basically the same team that had won the World Series from the year before, except for the trade that sent Dick Tracewski to the Detroit Tigers for Phil Regan. We called Phil "The Vulture," because he would swoop in and get the win in relief. In fact, he won a franchise record 13 games in a row that year. But I was still a little hobbled from the year before.

Spring training got off to a strange start when Don and Sandy held a joint holdout. They wanted raises, three-year deals that would pay them $500,000 total. And this was at a time when there were no agents like today, and the unofficial limit was $100,000 a year. Don and Sandy threatened to quit baseball altogether and become actors. They were going to make a movie called *Warning Shot* with David Janssen. But the day after they appeared on the movie set, they each signed one-year deals. Sandy got $125,000 and Don got $100,000. It ended up being about a $40,000 raise for Sandy and a $20,000 raise for Don. Not too bad.

While those two stayed away from a good portion of spring training, a door opened for a younger pitcher. Don Sutton, who was called "Sutton Death," made the team, even though he hadn't ever played at Triple-A. He had a great curveball and a lot of confidence. He ended up setting Dodgers' pitching records for most career wins (233), losses (181), games (550), strikeouts (2,696) and shutouts (52). But he got hurt in September and we could have definitely used him against the Orioles in the World Series.

7

RANDOM MUSINGS

Divine Intervention

Maury Wills may have always seemed to be cool and confident and in control on the field. And most of the time he was. But there was this one time when he nearly came unglued. We were at Crosley Field in Cincinnati playing the Reds. We were in the field, the bases were loaded and Frank Robinson came walking up to the plate. Maury was at shortstop and his knees started shaking and his hands began sweating. He was scared. So he called time out and, to pass the time, he looked back at me in left and, wouldn't you know it, he told me to move. That's all he could do because he was so scared.

Well, the ball always finds you when you don't want it, and sure enough, Frank hit a shot at Maury, a grounder that he somehow lost sight off. But it popped up and hit him in the chest. Maury says that what happened next was a "spiritual" experience.

"It popped right in front of me and just floated there," Maury said.

True, the ball could have gone to his left or to his right or through his legs or even over his head. But he says, to this day, that because it stayed in front of him, "floating," that someone was watching over him because he made the play and wasn't scared any more.

"If someone wonders if there's a God or not," Maury said, "have them come talk to me."

Painfully Spiritual

I had a similar experience, though I don't think it was spiritual as much as it was painful. I was playing third base—Maury likes to say it was because they couldn't find a position for me. There was probably some truth to that, because in 1961 I played 59 games at third base, 44 games in left field, 39 games in center field, and 30 games in right field. I played two different positions in 42 games and three different positions in three games.

This game, though, I was at the Hot Corner and Sandy was pitching. Well, they didn't tell me that Koufax was going to throw a change-up. So this batter just sits on the pitch and smokes this one-hopper to me at third that hit me square in the chest. It bounced in front of me and I threw him out. I looked over at Maury and I couldn't talk—nothing would come out because the ball knocked the wind out of me. And Koufax was like, "Are you all right?" I was fine as soon as I caught my breath.

Death Field

Baseball is full of superstitions and superstitious people. But it's not just superstition if it's real, right? According to Lou Johnson, left field must have been home to a black cat who broke a mirror on some Friday the 13th.

"Nobody wanted to play left field at one time," Lou recalled. "We called it Death Field. First, Tommy broke his ankle. Then I broke mine. And then, wouldn't you know it, Al Ferrara broke his. It seemed like we just had two centerfielders and a right fielder out there because no one wanted to go out there to left. We would have just shifted over if we could have."

Al Ferrara was actually my first replacement when I broke my ankle. But four days after Al took over, he broke a finger, which truly opened the door for Lou Johnson. Lou actually broke his thumb a month after coming up to the Dodgers, but he closed strong. His 12 home runs tied second baseman Jim Lefebvre, who was the National League's rookie of the year in 1965, for the team lead.

I Think I Just Killed a Guy

A couple of hours after a game in San Francisco, I was hanging out with Willie Davis in a hallway at the team hotel and Don Drysdale came walking by. He looked like he was in a serious daze as he looked at me and said, "I think I just killed a guy." So we're just looking at him like, "What?" And he said it again, "I think I just killed a guy." Then Don grabbed me by the throat to demonstrate what he was talking about. He was just crazy, grabbing me and tossing me about and I was saying, "Okay, Okay I get the picture."

I think Don was drunk. We never found out what he was talking about, though. He must have gotten in a fight at a bar or something.

Show Ron the Money

It was after one of Sandy Koufax's no-hitters that word of the no-no filtered to Don Drysdale, and Don's classic response was,

Ron Fairly, flanked by Dick Smith on the left and Wes Parker on the right, was a smooth-fielding first baseman as well as a good outfielder. He jokingly had issues with the notion that the high-paid Dodgers pitchers were "poor" because they had little or no offensive support.
Courtesy of the Los Angeles Dodgers

"That's great, but did he win?" We all got a kick out of that because we knew that our hitting was the weak link of the team. But Ron Fairly did not take too kindly to the jab that our pitchers were in a no-win situation.

"It bothered me that everyone said, 'Poor Dodger pitchers,'" Ron said. "Well hell, they were the ones who had all the money.

Don't tell me how poor they were. They were pitching in the best ballpark in the world to pitch in at Dodger Stadium. Don't tell me about them, they're making all the money. The poor Dodger hitters had to hit in this ballpark."

He makes a good point.

Sending the Pitchers Ahead

If we were playing a night game, and we had a day game the following afternoon in a different city, it was common practice to send our starting pitcher ahead of the rest of the team. The thinking was that getting him there early would give him the opportunity to get a good night's sleep because the team wouldn't be getting in until really late. But Ron Fairly remembers the strategy backfiring when we sent "Big Hurt" Stan Williams ahead to Chicago.

"The team got in at about two o'clock in the morning and we were checking in to the hotel and picking up our keys and here comes Stan, he was just getting in too," Ron said. "We had a tendency to get in trouble in Chicago because they played all the day games there."

I'm Going to Kill You

How crazy was Big Hurt, AKA Stan Williams? Well, Ron Fairly told me about this one time when he was playing first base, Willie Mays got a base hit off Stan and Stan was just glaring at him from the mound. Stan finally spoke and as he stared at him he said to Willie, "Before I finish playing this game, I'm going to kill you."

That was part of Stan's fear factor—his attempt to intimidate the opponent. And Willie looked at Ron and Willie said, in that high-pitched voice of his, "What the hell did I do?" Willie's still alive and kicking. Mostly these days he watches on as his godson, Barry

Bonds, chases Hank Aaron's all-time home run record of 755 homers in San Francisco.

A Nice Debut

I made my major league debut by striking out. Other guys have made much better, and much longer-lasting, impressions in their first appearance in a major league uniform.

It did not take relief pitcher Pete Richert long to make his mark. In his first major league game, against the Cincinnati Reds on April 12, 1962, the lefty struck out the first six batters he faced to set a franchise record for most consecutive strikeouts by a reliever. He still holds that record, though Ron Perranoski tied the mark against the New York Mets on September 12, 1966.

Go Home, Moose

Moose Skowron is the first to admit that he struggled mightily in his lone season in a Dodger uniform. And if he didn't want to face facts then, all he had to do was listen to the crowd at Dodger Stadium.

"There was this one guy in the stands who used to always yell, 'Go home, Moose. Go home. Go back to New York.' And he was right," Moose said, "I was lousy."

But after beating his former team, the Yankees, in the World Series, and having a good series by batting .385 with a home run and three RBIs, the heckler was strangely silent.

"I didn't hear him then," Moose recalled. "I wish to hell that I would have found him. I would have said, 'Hello.'"

I hope that's all Moose would have done to that guy.

Like Death Warmed Over

Nate Oliver tried to help out a friend in an opposing clubhouse before a Sandy Koufax start. Or maybe he was just trying to use a little psychological warfare.

"It was a Sunday game at Atlanta and Sandy was scheduled to pitch, but he came down with a real bad 24-hour virus," Nate remembers. "His eyes were all red and rolling up into the back of his head and he was all pale. He just looked like death warmed over.

"Our lockers were a couple away from each other and Sandy looked at me and said, 'Brute, I've only had a couple hours of sleep.' So I asked him if he was going to be able to pitch and he said he wasn't sure. So we took batting practice and we came back in and I asked him again and he still wasn't sure. It was about 11 in the morning, the game was at 1, and we went out for infield practice. After coming back in, I asked again. This time, though, I asked the trainer if Sandy was going to toe the rubber and he wasn't sure.

"So it's getting late, about 12:20 and the game starts at 1 and Sandy decides he's going to give it a go. Only one other time had I seen Sandy looking like that when he pitched. So I ran out of our clubhouse, down the corridor to the Braves' clubhouse and I asked the clubbie to get me Mack Jones. Mack was my friend because we came up through the minors together. I told him that Sandy looked like death warmed over and that the last time I seen him like that he had scattered maybe two, three, four hits. I told Mack that Sandy was likely to do that again, and if Mack was wise, he would grab one of those hits.

"Well, Mack slammed the door in my face. So in Mack's first at-bat he gets a curve and strikes out. In this second at-bat Mack gets a curve and strikes out. In his third at-bat Mack gets a curve and strikes out. And in the ninth inning, Mack was the last batter with two outs and he gets another curveball and he strikes out. We won, 2-1, and Sandy gave up maybe four hits. I tried to tell Mack at the time that he could have taken the opportunity to grab one of those hits, but he chose not to."

Who says you should never fraternize with the enemy?

Reliving Sandy's No-No's

Every one of Sandy Koufax's four no-hitters had a special moment or a special play that gave it added significance. That he threw one in four straight years only made the accomplishment that much more amazing.

Sandy's first no-no came on Saturday, June 30, 1962, at Dodger Stadium. Sandy knew he was on to something special when he struck out the first three batters of the game . . . on nine pitches! Nine pitches. Amazing.

I had something to do with helping along his second no-hitter, on Saturday, May 11, 1963. It was again at Dodger Stadium and we were playing the San Francisco Giants. Juan Marichal was pitching for the Giants and in the seventh inning, Felipe Alou hit a shot into the left field corner. I got on my horse and snagged the ball just before it hit the wall.

"It doesn't surprise me," Sandy told a reporter about my catch. "You always need help to throw a no-hitter."

As bad as I was on defense, I was just glad to help.

Sandy's third no-no was Thursday, June 4, 1964. It was Sandy's only no-no on the road; he pulled it off at the Philadelphia Phillies' Connie Mack Stadium.

No-hitter No. 4 was the most special of all, mostly because it was a perfect game and the guy pitching against us, the Chicago Cubs' Bob Hendley, threw a one-hitter at us. It was Thursday, September 9, 1965, and the Cubs were in town in the heat of a pennant race. Five teams were within four games of each other for first place that day and we were tied for second with the Cincinnati Reds, a half-game behind the Giants.

We got our run in the fifth inning without getting a hit. Lou Johnson walked and was sacrificed to second base by Ron Fairly. Lou then stole third base, but on the play, the Cubs' rookie catcher, Chris Krug, threw the ball into left field, which allowed Lou to score. That was all we would get. And it was all we would need.

"My control was real good," Sandy was quoted as saying after the game. "My curve was the best I've had all year. And in the last three innings, the fast ball was my best pitch."

Jeff Torborg was in his second year with the Dodgers and he caught the game and made his way through the crowd of reporters to get Sandy's autograph after the game.

"I didn't have to shake him off very often," Sandy said after the game.

Torborg gave all the credit to Sandy.

"I didn't do anything but catch the ball all night, but what a thrill. I dropped one pitch but that was a curve in the dirt. Sandy had command all the time."

Lou had the only hit of the game, a double that came in the seventh inning. Until then, reporters were busy scrambling in the press box, trying to figure out the last time a double-no-hitter had happened. It happened on May 2, 1917, and was thrown by Cincinnati's Fred Toney and Chicago's James Vaughn. Both threw no-hitters for nine innings but the Reds got a pair of hits in the 10th and beat Vaughn, 1-0.

The Steal Sign

Ron Fairly gave new meaning to the terms "all-nighter" and "sloshball." After we had clinched the 1965 pennant on the next-to-last day of the season, Alston told Ron to go ahead and go out and celebrate that night because he wasn't going to be in the lineup the next day for the season finale anyway.

"So I hooked up with Drysdale and two or three other guys, and by the time I got to the ballpark the next morning for the day game I hadn't been to bed yet," Ron said. "I saw my name was in the lineup so I asked Alston, 'What's this?' He said that Wes Parker had an upset stomach or something and couldn't play. I was in. That was an adventure.

"Well, Alston had come to an agreement with Vin Scully that he would act as the manager for the game because we had already clinched the pennant. Vinny would not only broadcast but manage. They set up a line from the broadcast booth to the dugout so Vinny's broadcasting his moves to the fans. When I came up, I even told the pitcher, 'Don't try to finesse me because I'm going to swing at everything anyway.' Lo and behold I got a base hit.

"So I'm on first base and Vinny decides to have some fun. With all the transistor radios in the stadium I could here Vinny's voice. He said, 'Ron doesn't steal too many bases so let's send him.' Vinny didn't know the condition I was in. Sure enough, I look over at Preston Gomez coaching at third base and he gives me the steal sign. So I go. And I make it. Then I hear Vinny say, 'I bet the Braves wouldn't expect Ron to steal on two pitches in a row.' Preston Gomez gave me the steal sign again. I took off and the ball was fouled off. I get back to second base and he gives me the sign again. The third time I just shook my head and said no. Vinny's laughing, and so is the crowd.

"I didn't care, we were going to the World Series. I mean, good golly, I haven't even been to bed yet and, Holy Cow, I'm in the lineup."

Go! Go! Go!

No one felt worse than Maury Wills after he was traded away to the Pittsburgh Pirates following his Japanese tour misadventure. And he probably hit rock bottom when he was left unprotected and selected by the expansion Montreal Expos. But you can bet his spirits picked up a bit when he came back to the Dodgers in a 1969 trade for Ron Fairly. In his heyday, Maury was the center of attention and he loved to disrupt the other team's rhythm, just by dancing on the basepaths. Whenever he got on base, the crowd used to chant, "Go! Go! Go!" And he was gone. He may have set the Dodgers' single-season mark for getting caught 35 times in 1965, but by the time he retired after the 1972 season, Maury had set the franchise's all-time steals record with 490 stolen bases. He still holds it.

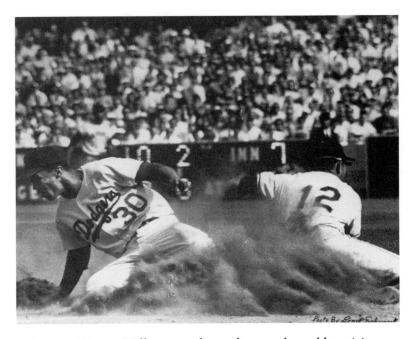

Whenever Maury Wills got on base, the crowd would anticipate a stolen base by chanting, "Go, Go, Go," especially during his MVP season of 1962 when he set a major league record with 104 steals. Here's his 104th theft, against the Giants. Courtesy of the Los Angeles Dodgers

The Brooklyn Bridge?

When the Dodgers played their final game in Brooklyn in 1957, Sandy Koufax was the last Dodger pitcher to throw a pitch in the borough. And when the Dodgers returned to New York to play the expansion Mets in 1962, Sandy was the first L.A. Dodger to pitch in Gotham. I guess you could say that Sandy bridged two eras. Does that make him a Brooklyn bridge, of sorts? That title probably fits better on the Mets, who played their first two seasons at the Polo Grounds in Harlem before moving to Shea Stadium in Queens in 1964. After all, the Mets' color scheme of blue and orange comes from the two teams that left New York—the Dodgers and Giants.

Say Cheese!

Andy Carey was a reserve infielder who only played with us for one year, in 1962; but he made quite an impression. Not with his glove or with his bat, but with his camera. Andy was an amateur photographer who brought his camera everywhere. He used to take candid shots and he also staged some pictures. One that comes to mind showed the different aspects of our team. He had Maury sliding into second base, Don and Sandy on their follow through, as if they had just pitched a ball, and me standing there holding a bat. He probably could have named the picture "The speed, the heat and the bat."

Another crazy shot had us all dressed up in the clubhouse after a game. Some say we looked like the Village People. Maury was wearing a pirate hat and an eye patch and holding a base. Don had a fake arrow going through his head and fake, bugged-out eye balls and he was wearing what looked like an old F-Troop hat while winding up Maury like he was some wind-up toy. I was wearing a derby hat and leopard-print boxers, Ron Fairly had on an Indian headdress and Frank Howard wore a bald skin cap and a T-Shirt that read, "Mr. Clean."

The way Ron described it, we were staging a picture to show what a base thief Maury was.

"If we had won in 1962," Ron said, "I can't even imagine what kind of picture we would have taken."

Hooray for Hollywood

You can easily see the Hollywood sign from the top of Dodger Stadium. So it only makes sense that so many Dodgers crossed over to the entertainment world. Sandy and Don were big enough that during their joint holdout in 1966 they threatened to quit baseball altogether and become actors. While Sandy was in *Mr. Ed*, Don appeared in *The Flying Nun*. And they both showed up in westerns.

Maury was always in Las Vegas performing, and I performed in a few shows. Wes Parker even appeared on *The Brady Bunch* as himself before making it as a full-time actor after he retired. Jim Lefebvre, who won the National League's rookie of the year award in 1965, made his mark on *Batman*. He played one of the Riddler's henchmen, a guy named Across, who gets beat up by the Caped Crusader and the Boy Wonder.

Frenchy, that was Jim Lefebvre's nickname, also appeared as a headhunter, along with Al Ferrara, on *Gilligan's Island*. When he was a kid, Jim was a batboy for the Dodgers at the Coliseum. In 2003, Frenchy assumed his greatest role when he was named manager of the Chinese national baseball team for the Asian championships. Not even Hollywood could have come up with a script like that.

A Rookie Mistake

Wes Parker came up for good in 1964, and it was during spring training that he says he made a typical rookie mistake—all because of me.

"We were playing Kansas City in an exhibition game and Tommy didn't start," Wes said. "So he came in later and hit a pinch-hit home run to win the game. And I said, 'Gee, maybe we should have Tommy come off the bench all the time.' There was silence. It was like they were saying, 'Uh, no, rookie. Tommy Davis does not come off the bench.' What a rookie move."

Switching It Up

Wes was a smooth-fielding first baseman who won six straight Gold Gloves and made up one-fourth of the Dodgers' all switch-hitting infield in 1965 and 1966. That infield also included second baseman Jim Lefebvre, third baseman Jim Gilliam and shortstop Maury Wills.

"We never thought about it," Wes said. "It wasn't until the World Series against the Twins that we realized it, because someone came up to us and asked us to take a picture, with each of us holding a bat over each shoulder."

Maury, Lefebvre and Wes all had something else in common— they all homered from both sides of the plate in a single game, though not the same game. In fact, Wes is still the only L.A. Dodger to hit for the cycle. He did it on May 7, 1970 against the Mets at Shea Stadium. Even then, the moment was lost on Wes.

"I had never heard the term 'cycle' before," Wes said, "so I had no idea what it was. But you need more luck than skill to pull it off. You need skill to hit the ball but you need luck to get each kind of hit."

8

OLD SCHOOL

Payback's a Pain

We were playing Milwaukee and Lew Burdette was pitching for the Braves. I hit one foul a long ways. I pulled it and I was looking at it and admiring it. I got back in the box and I could see Burdette saying something, just mumbling and looking all mean as he took the mound to pitch again. And it looked like he was looking at me, but I wasn't sure. So I glanced back at Del Crandall, their catcher, and I said, "Del, is he talking to me?" Del didn't know what to say so he just said all innocently, "Well, I don't know."

He knew. The next pitch nailed me right in the neck. Now I was a little mad. It was early in the game so I didn't want to run out there and charge the mound. So I went to first base, steaming. That pitch was close to my head, and you don't mess with the head.

The ball was hit to shortstop and they tried to turn a double play. I slid into second base and I put my spike into Frank Bolling's shin. I think I put him out for the rest of the year. Bolling was a nice guy, so it wasn't really anything against him.

The game was played harder back then, and taking out a fielder trying to turn a play was accepted, so long as it was a clean play. Here, I took out Mets shortstop Roy McMillan. Courtesy of the Los Angeles Dodgers

And after I got up from the slide, I ran right across the mound and nobody said anything to me. That's the way we played in those days. I mean, he hit me in my neck and I'm just going to take it? I don't think so. There was no retaliation after I spiked Bolling, because it was over. Getting hit in those days was a common occurrence. Pitchers threw at hitters all the time, and hitters had to retaliate to protect themselves.

Fairly Fair Game for Gibson

Ron Fairly was not as lucky as I was when it came to having success against Bob Gibson. And all Ron did was get a few base hits off him.

"Bob was such a fierce competitor that if you weren't wearing the same uniform he was, he didn't like you," Ron said, and was he ever right. "One game against the Cardinals, I got two base hits against him, and as I came to the plate for the third time, I looked back at Joe Torre, who was catching, and all I could see were his dark eyes behind that catcher's mask. I told him, 'I'm not going to like this at-bat.' Sure enough, Bob drilled me.

"As I was getting up and dusting myself off, I looked back at Torre and this time all I could see were his teeth, smiling through his catcher's mask."

I wonder what would have happened had Ron hit a couple of game-winning homers off Gibson.

Hanging With the Say Hey Kid

It would be the understatement of the century to say that the Dodgers and Giants didn't like each other. It was a feud that went back to when both teams played in New York—the Dodgers in

Brooklyn and the Giants in Harlem—and continued on to California.

They had their stadium first, Candlestick Park, but nobody wanted to go there because it was so damn cold. The winds at Candlestick were crazy. The air in the infield would blow differently than the air that blew the flags in the outfield.

We always fought with Willie Mays during a game, but we hung out afterwards. Man, we would fight like crazy. But after playing the Giants in San Francisco we'd go out with Willie to get something to eat and drink. He'd take us all over the city because he practically owned it. Then we'd head over to his house. Willie had hundreds of those Alpaca sweaters that were popular back then. He had hundreds of them, because he got everything for free. We'd go over to his house and I'd take two, three, four of those sweaters because we were about the same size anyhow. He'd get mad and in that high-pitched voice of his, he would yell, "Hey, man, get out of there. What are you doing? Get out of my damn closet. Give me back my damn sweater." Then we'd go to the ballpark and he'd still be screaming shit, "Don't be going through my closet no more." Then he'd go out and kick our ass during the game.

After the game he'd come over and be like, "C'mon, where are we going to eat?" and he'd take us some place to drink. It was the same thing all over again. Good thing the Dodger fans didn't know we were hanging out with the enemy.

The Good Old Days

Reporters and the press in general were different when I was coming up. Way different. Back then, the sportswriters mingled with the ballplayers a little better and hung out with some of them after the games. They didn't write then like they do now. Vin Scully, who's seen it all, has a theory as to why things got flipped around.

"The media has changed dramatically," Vin said. "In the old days, everybody wrote the game—who, what, when, why, where and how. I mean, that was the way you did it. Then television came along. So by 10 o'clock, 11 o'clock at night, most people knew what happened. So now the newspaper guy had to write an angle for the afternoon paper, and that's how it started—the exposés, the ugliness."

One reporter had to have a different story than another. That was and remains the competition factor.

Those Guys Are Good

Very few players are able to spend their entire career with one team. And even though I was traded by the Dodgers, I still consider myself a Dodger at heart. That's why it was so fun to play in Old-Timer's Games as a Dodger after retiring from the game. Ron Fairly and I played together in one game against the San Francisco Giants in Phoenix, and he said he remembered me being in awe of our opponents.

"When they introduced us, we were standing along the first-base line," Ron said, "and when they introduced the Giants they had Felipe Alou. They had Willie Mays. They had Willie McCovey. They had Orlando Cepeda. They had all these players and Tommy was standing next to me and he looked over and he said, 'Those guys are good. Look at that lineup. Those guys are really good.' So we played the game and we beat them.

"Standing in the shower after the game, I said, 'Tommy, you're right. Those guys that we played today, they were good. But we beat them again. We weren't too bad, either.'"

I would have traded that Old-Timer's Game win for a victory against the Giants in 1962.

Runnin' In the Night

During spring training, the pitching coaches set up a system of nets to help the pitchers work on their pinpoint control. It was an intricate system of strings and nets that covered a good amount of ground on one side of the field. In the center of the nets was a small opening that the pitchers were supposed to throw the ball through. The opening represented the strike zone. Fresco Thompson's head nearly went through that opening one time.

It was a late night during spring training when Fresco, who was our director of minor league operations, saw some players coming in late and breaking curfew. Fresco was hiding out, trying to catch the guys, and he saw pitcher Larry Sherry. But Larry saw Fresco, too, so he took off running into the darkness with Fresco in hot pursuit. Fresco was yelling at Larry, "I'm going to get . . ." But before he could get out the last word, Fresco ran, full speed, into a net, right at neck level. He almost choked himself. Larry and his guys got away, for at least one night anyway.

Another time, Roy Hartsfield, a minor league coach, was running late at night after a kid who was at Dodgertown on a try-out basis. Hartsfield said he didn't want to catch the kid to punish him. He wanted to sign him because he was so fast.

It's Coming

If Maury was on base when you were at bat, you knew a fastball away was coming sooner or later, because the catcher needed to get a good pitch to try to throw him out. Sometimes Maury would steal bases when we were up big in a game. That was just the way he played. That's when you knew the other pitcher was going to throw at you. You were like, "Oh shit." But we had pitchers who would protect us, too. And if the pitchers didn't, then John Roseboro would from behind the plate. He protected Maury so well that one time he set off the ugliest fight in major league baseball history.

The Roseboro-Marichal Affair

I was at home trying to recover from my ankle injury, but the Dodgers were in San Francisco in the dog days of summer playing the Giants. Who knew that a riot was about to break out? It's no secret that the Dodgers and Giants did not get along and that there were many beanball wars between the two teams. But on this day—August 22, 1965—things got real wild.

The Giants said it started in the first game of the series. They claimed that Maury pulled his bat back into their catcher's mask to get a free base on a catcher's interference call. Well, in the series finale, Juan Marichal was pitching for the Giants and he took matters into his own hands. First he dusted Maury. Then he did the same to Ron Fairly. Sandy Koufax was pitching for us, but he didn't play that way. He didn't need to always hit batters or brush them back.

But Johnny Roseboro did . . . from behind the plate. With Marichal batting, Johnny buzzed Marichal with his throw back to Sandy and the two exchanged words at the plate. Next thing you know, Marichal was clubbing Johnny over the head with his bat. All hell broke loose, and even Tito Fuentes, who was on deck, rushed in and started lifting his bat.

Meanwhile, I was at home in L.A., watching it all on the tube. I got up and I charged the TV. I went toward the TV, I don't know why. I got up like I was going to fight somebody and my wife at that time said, "What are you doing?" So I snapped out of it and said, "Oh, I don't know."

It was a 14-minute riot scene at Candlestick Park. Willie Mays thought that Johnny's eye came out of its socket—there was so much

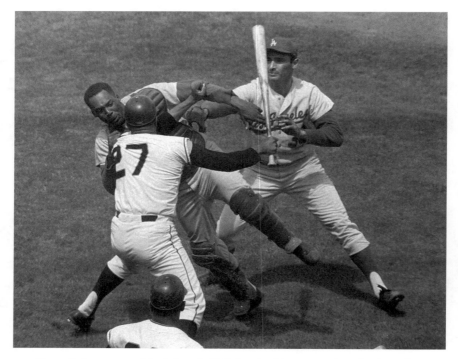

One of the most wicked baseball fights in history occurred when the Giants' Juan Marichal hit Johnny Roseboro over the head with a bat. I was watching the game at home but I still rushed the T.V. set when it happened. AP/WWP

blood. He ended up with a two-inch gash, 14 stitches and a lawsuit that was not settled for almost 10 years. Johnny sued Marichal for $110,000 but settled for $7,500.

People were just as upset at the weak penalty Marichal received from the National League president Warren Giles. He only fined Marichal $1,750 and suspended him eight games for what he called an "unprovoked and obnoxious" attack. Johnny recovered nicely. After taking a few days off, he had an 11-game hitting streak.

It took a while for Johnny and Marichal to make up, though they did. When Marichal was elected into the Hall of Fame in 1983, one of the first people he called was Johnny and they shared a good cry. And when Johnny died after a stroke in 2002, Marichal was at the funeral. Marichal is a good man. He just did something bad that one day. Strangely enough, Marichal retired as a Dodger, in 1975.

Moose Blows Kisses

Moose Skowron only spent one year with the Dodgers, but it was a memorable one. He was a major reason we swept the Yankees in the 1963 World Series . . . a year after the Yankees traded him to the Dodgers. But the year before coming to L.A., Moose had been part of a championship team in the Bronx.

"In the 1962 World Series I had a triple and a single against Juan Marichal when we played the San Francisco Giants," Moose said. "Pitchers don't forget. They'll either get you the next at-bat or the next year. So sure enough, when I'm with the Dodgers, I'm struggling and only hitting .210 early in the season. But Marichal knocked me down. In the next inning, Willie Mays came up to bat for the Giants and Sandy knocked his ass down. I just said, 'Sandy, I love you.' I blew kisses to him."

That's how the game was played.

How Do You Feel?

Being a relief pitcher for the Dodgers in the 1960s seemed like an easy enough job. With workhorses like Sandy Koufax and Don Drysdale eating up all the innings, the relievers would have a little more fun than usual the night before one of their starts. Especially if Sandy was pitching and especially if we were in Chicago, where we only played day games.

Ron Fairly said he remembered one specific incident when the relievers partied a little too much the night before a Koufax start, thinking they wouldn't be needed the next afternoon.

"We got to the second inning, and we had Pete Richert warming up in the bullpen," Ron said. "Sandy was struggling in the third inning and Alston came out to the mound and he asked Sandy, 'How do you feel?' Sandy said, 'Better than the guy you have warming up.' And there's Pete, just wiped out in the bullpen, trying to get it going. Alston ended up turning around and walking back to the dugout and sure enough, Sandy ended up going seven or eight innings, and I think we won the ballgame."

Stop the Bus

Walt Alston was a former schoolteacher in Ohio who liked people to think that he was the quiet farm-boy type. And most of the time he was. But when he got pissed, watch out. He didn't take any guff. In fact, he often challenged players to fight. There's that classic story that he challenged Jackie Robinson once.

"Walt was big enough and he was strong enough," Ron Fairly said.

Alston was about six foot two and 210 pounds. But he also once challenged the whole team to a fight. It was a month into the 1963 season, and we had just lost three of four to the Pirates in Pittsburgh. We were in seventh place with a record of 12-14, so we weren't in the best of moods. On the way to the airport afterward, we were on this old, broken-down bus that seemed to be crawling. Then the Pirates flew by us on a brand-new bus because they were flying out of town, too. So we started yelling at Lee Scott, our traveling secretary. We were saying things like, "Why don't you get a goddamned bus that goes faster?"

So Alston said, "All right, get off of him. Leave him alone." But we didn't. Alston had enough. He ordered the bus driver to pull over

Walt Alston (left) didn't exactly see eye to eye with all of his players, myself included—especially when he wanted to trade me. Or, when he stopped the team bus and challenged us all to a fist fight. Talk about Old School. Courtesy of the Los Angeles Dodgers

and then he challenged us all. He said if we didn't like the bus, we could meet him outside. He went out and paced around. No one took him up on his offer. A lot of the guys thought that was the turning point for the season.

Facing a Legend

We were playing the Giants early in my career, and Sad Sam Jones was going to pitch against us. He was a legend among the black ballplayers. In his first year with the Giants he led the National League with 21 victories and a 2.83 earned run average. To this day he is one of just 11 black pitchers ever to have won at least 20 games in a major league baseball season. During pregame warmups Jim Gilliam was talking to him off to the side—they were good friends—and as I walked by, Gilliam pointed at me and told Sam, "This young guy, he's a pretty good hitter. He's going to get some hits off you."

He was just egging him on. But Sam didn't get the joke, I guess. So Sam looked at me and real calmly he said, "Young fella, I'm going to hit you." I just stopped in my tracks and took a deep breath and said, "But, Mr. Jones, I didn't do nothing."

9

RACE RELATIONS

Sweet Lou Speaks

A reporter once asked Lou Johnson, "Why does the black player swing so hard?" It didn't take Lou long to come up with an answer, "Because the ball is white." Lou always said, "No other race went through what we had to go through. We laughed to keep from crying."

Lou was born in 1934 in the Deep South—Lexington, Kentucky—so he saw segregation and the Civil Rights movement up close and personal and it impacted the way he saw the world then as well as how he sees it now.

"I'm speaking to you as a Negro," Lou told a reporter. "Jesse Jackson has me as an African-American now and I don't know what he and the Rainbow Coalition will have me designated as next. I just hope he doesn't run for president again, because who knows what the hell I'll be called then."

Lou also thinks the game and the players from our era are much different from today's game and players.

Sweet Lou Johnson (right) celebrating another clutch home run with Ron Fairly, talked with both his well-traveled bat and his mouth when he came to the Dodgers in 1965. Lou took over as my replacement after I broke my right ankle. AP/WWP

"Everybody could smoke that ball back then," Lou said. "And guys were pitching nine innings."

Sandy Relates

Sandy faced a lot of stuff when he first came up and it affected him a little bit. Because he signed for over $4,000 and he had to stay on the major league roster for two years, a lot of the guys, from what I heard, said he was taking someone else's spot. And being Jewish, he knows what it is to be discriminated against a little bit. He went through hell. That's why he hung out with the brothers.

But he took it real good, and all that did was give him more inspiration. That's why he struck out a lot of guys. He also related well to the black guys on the team. Wouldn't you, if you knew that they were the nucleus of the team? I mean, think about it—they did-n't have too many black players back then who were bench players. Either you were good or you had to leave. You didn't sit around. Wes Covington established himself, and then he became a good pinch hitter. But there weren't too many black players who sat on the bench. Either you started or you went back down to the minors or moved on to another organization or went home.

Think about it in terms of the Dodgers back then. Maury Wills and Jim Gilliam were both really important parts of that team. Willie Davis played. I played. Roseboro played. Who's sitting on the bench who's black? No one. So wouldn't you relate to the black play-ers if you were Koufax?

I Was a Little Stunned

Al Campanis was the man who signed me to my first profes-sional contract, so I took it a little hard when he said the things he said on ABC's *Nightline* show. It was in April of 1987 when he was on the show to mark the 40th anniversary of Jackie Robinson break-ing the color barrier. Al and Jackie had even roomed together as players back then.

But when Ted Koppel asked Al why there were no black man-agers or general managers in baseball at the time, his answers seemed to take on a racist tone. When Koppel asked if there was prejudice in baseball, Al answered, "No, I don't believe it's prejudice. I truly believe that [blacks] may not have some of the necessities to be, let's say, a field manager, or perhaps a general manager."

Al Campanis was the man who signed me, so I took it a little hard when he made his racially insensitive remarks about blacks on ABC's Nightline *in April, 1987. Here, Al (center) is giving me and Willie Davis (right) instructions during our early playing days.* Courtesy of the Los Angeles Dodgers

I was a little stunned. Whatever point he was trying to make did not get across. He was fired within two days. A lot of people at the time wondered how I felt about his remarks, but I couldn't jump on him because he signed me so I just said, "Hey, he's been very fair to me, gives me a lot of respect, never had any problems with him." But he made his comments in front of seven million people on live television. And he took a lot of heat for them.

I didn't jump on the bandwagon. I just know the facts. But his comments about blacks lacking necessities—they really hurt. I didn't like that at all. That killed me. That was the worst thing he could have said. He was sort of snooty. He had an uppity attitude about him, but I didn't think it was racial at the time. But hey, he said what he said. And the commentator, Koppel, tried to let him get out, and he wouldn't do it.

Segregation Within the Stadium

Early in my days with the Dodgers they still had black and white drinking fountains for fans in the stands at Holman Stadium in Vero Beach. They also had the black and white bathrooms and the black people sat in right field. Willie Davis, Jim Gilliam, Johnny Roseboro and I went over to Peter O'Malley, who was running the spring training complex at the time, and said, "Peter, Jackie Robinson integrated this thing in 1947, and we still have a problem at Holman Stadium, right now in 1961."

He kind of said, "What?" It didn't dawn on him at the time. But to his credit, the next day everything was gone. They white-washed all that stuff. And we had to physically take the black people to seat them in other spots around the stadium. When we had an exhibition game we went and took the people out of the right field area and told them to sit in left field, sit behind home plate, sit over there. And they wouldn't believe us.

"Oh no, we can't do that," they said. So we just took them and told them to sit wherever they wanted to from now on. That was the integration of Holman Stadium.

Looking For the Links

When it came to golf, we couldn't play anywhere in Vero Beach. Nowhere. At least not the black guys on the team. The first place that let us play was in Stuart, Florida. And that was like 45 minutes to an hour south of our spring training complex. So after playing we'd have to drive really fast back to Vero Beach. Then the next place that let us play was in Melbourne. But that was just as far away, just in the opposite direction.

Remember, we were in the South. Mr. O'Malley knew that we liked to play golf, so he built us a nine-hole golf course at Vero Beach. Well, it was for everybody, but we played on that course so much it felt like it was built for us, meaning the black guys in the Dodger organization. The best thing about it, though, was it kept us in Vero Beach, because if we kept driving all over Florida searching for golf courses that would let us play, sooner or later, somebody would have gotten in trouble.

Clearing Out Chavez Ravine

I was still in the minor leagues when a big controversy erupted in Chavez Ravine, where Dodger Stadium was going to be built. It was early in the 1959 season when pictures ran in the newspapers showing residents being forcefully taken out of their houses there by sheriff's deputies. The people that lived there were primarily Latinos and they said that they had lived there for generations. That left a sour taste in a lot of people's mouths. I didn't like the fact that a lot of the people were complaining about having to leave. I kind of felt bad for them, but I wasn't in a position to say anything. When you displace people, and they're complaining about it, ordinarily you'd put them in a place of equal value. A lot of people are still upset today about how the Dodgers got the land for Dodger Stadium.

A Stolen Asterisk?

When Maury Wills started closing in on Ty Cobb's stolen base record in 1962 it caused a lot of drama. The commissioner of baseball, Ford Frick, talked about how if Maury didn't pass Cobb's mark of 96 steals in 154 games—that's what Cobb did it in in 1915—then he'd put an asterisk on Maury's name in the record book. That didn't sit too well with Maury, and a lot of people thought it smacked of racism, especially because Cobb was credited with two extra stolen bases in tie games that year.

After 154 games, Maury had stolen 94 bases, and he was a little bitter at the commissioner. Maury even said that he wished he had known the commissioner was going to change the rules in midstream, cause if he had known, he would have gone for more steals earlier in the season.

The funny thing was, Frick backed off, and after playing that three-game playoff with the Giants, Maury ended up with 104 steals in 165 games. And there was no asterisk to be found.

Not the Same Leverage

The same spring that Sandy and Don held out together, Maury did the same, just on his own. But because he was by himself, he didn't have the same leverage. Maury was making $60,000 and he wanted $100,000, what was then considered the unofficial max. There was a story going around at the time that Buzzie told Maury that Mr. O'Malley would blackball him. The feeling was that a black man did have the same leverage as two white pitchers. Maury got a raise, though, and he signed for $75,000.

Lost in Translation

I played winter ball in Venezuela in 1958. Two of my teammates were the Sherry brothers—Larry, who was a pitcher, and Norm, who was a catcher. Larry learned to throw a slider in Venezuela. And we all learned that the press in a black Latin nation took things literally.

According to *The Sporting News*, the Sherrys were the 10th pitcher-catcher battery of brothers in baseball history. One game in Venezuela, Larry and Norm got in an argument during the game and the next day the newspapers said, "Hermanos luchando," or, brothers fighting.

We Couldn't Swim

Pete Reiser was our manager in Venezuela, a black nation. Venezuela is a Latin nation, but the people there are black. We were staying at this hotel called the Del Lago Hotel. Pete and I took our wives to the swimming pool at the hotel, but they wouldn't let us swim. Now this is a black nation. But the hotel manager was from Texas and he had this policy that wouldn't let us swim.

So Pete went off. He said, "You've got to be kidding me. My wife can't swim because she's Jewish, right? No, no, we're leaving. But if you ever come to a game, if I see you, I'm going to throw you out of the stadium. Because I don't like you."

I was relieved that Pete had my back like that, and I just said to myself, "Go on, Pete."

The Watts Riots

I was still out injured when Sandy threw his perfect game. But I was in the stadium. There was a small crowd that night and a weird vibe and there was the smell of smoke in the air because the Watts riots were still dying down. When I drove to the game, it was like a ghost town in L.A. because nobody was out and police barricades were all over the city. I lived in Baldwin Hills at that time and I had to go all the way around the city to La Cienega just to get to Dodger Stadium. There were fires all over the place. You would have thought a bomb went off.

10

HEARTBREAK

The Collapse of '62

We had such a good team in 1962. We had a good formula—pitching plus speed plus timely hitting. We scored an L.A. franchise-record 842 runs that season and stole an L.A.-record 198 bases, more than half of which came courtesy of Maury. Those positives more than made up for our bad defense. Our team fielding percentage of .970 set a record that still stands today for the worst fielding Dodger team in L.A. We committed an L.A. Dodger record 193 errors.

It was our first year at Dodger Stadium, which was a prototypical pitcher's park, and we were so good all around that the odds-makers in Las Vegas had us as two-to-one favorites to win the National League pennant. I won the first of my two NL batting titles with a .346 batting average, and I also led the league with 230 hits and 153 RBIs, both of which are still Dodger single-season records. Before the season, Maury was quoted as saying that we should be the favorites and that were going to run away with the pennant. He made a runaway of the stolen base race, all right, break-

Little did we know when we posed for this picture at Spring Training in 1962 that we'd be the greatest Dodger team to never win a World Series, thanks to our epic collapse down the stretch that season. We won an L.A.-record 102 games that year, but did not go to the Fall Classic.
Courtesy of the Los Angeles Dodgers

ing Ty Cobb's record for steals with 104 thefts en route to being named the National League's Most Valuable Player. Don Drysdale won the Cy Young Award with a 25-9 record, 2.84 earned-run average and 232 strikeouts.

We should have been in the World Series against the Yankees. But that would have to wait.

That 1962 season was the first year that Sandy Koufax's arm really started bothering him. It bothered him enough that he missed several starts late in the summer. We had a four-game lead with seven games to play and then we blew it. After finishing with a record of 101-61, we had to play our rivals from Northern California, the same guys who came west with us from New York, the Giants, in a best-of-three playoff for the right to play the Yankees in the Fall Classic.

The Playoff

We lost six of our last seven games that year, and 10 of our final 13. But the one that hurt the most was on the final day of the season. That's when the St. Louis Cardinals beat us, 1-0, on a home run by their catcher, Gene Oliver. The Giants beat Houston, 2-1, on a Willie Mays homer. So they caught us to force the playoff. The Giants were so happy with Gene Oliver that they invited him to the World Series as their guest of honor.

We were still down emotionally when the first game of the playoff began at Candlestick Park, and the Giants took advantage, beating us, 8-0, even though Sandy Koufax started for us. It was the third straight game we had been shut out and Vin Scully remembered the Giants pulling some shenanigans to give them an edge.

"They watered the infield up there in San Francisco to stop Wills (slow him down on the basepaths)," Vin said. "And when they came down here to L.A., I don't know who it was, they gave out 10,000 duck calls to make fun of the Giants for wetting the infield down. So when the Giants came in, everybody's blowing these duck calls. Alvin Dark was the San Francisco manager and he had been a college football player at LSU. During the Revolutionary War, there was a general named Francis Marion, and he opened the dikes in Louisiana to screw up the British and he was called the Swamp Fox. I called Alvin Dark 'The Swamp Fox' for flooding the infield." I loved it when Vin made those kinds of comparisons.

We were still struggling with the bats in Game 2 at Dodger Stadium and we were behind 5-0 in the sixth inning when we woke up in time to rally for an 8-7 win. We were back and with Johnny Podres starting the rubber game, we figured we had it made. Especially when I hit a home run in the sixth inning to give us a 3-2 lead in the third game. We were up 4-2 in the ninth and only three outs away from going to the World Series against the Yankees when Ed Roebuck relieved Johnny on the hill. All hell was about to break loose.

Matty Alou led off with a single. Seemed harmless enough. And when Harvey Kuenn hit a one-hopper to Maury at short it seemed like a tailor-made double-play grounder. But it took our second baseman, Larry Burright, too long to get to the bag and he couldn't turn two. Because Larry was so far away from second to complete the force, Maury didn't know whether to run over to second himself or wait for Larry to come all the way over. So Maury threw the ball to him at second, but because he got there so late, Larry had to catch the ball, jump up and turn around to throw the ball to first all in one motion.

"He had to run like mad just to get back to get the force out and [then he] couldn't turn the double play," Ron Fairly remembered. "He had no chance."

Still, Burright barely missed getting Harvey at first base. And from there, the Giants scored all their runs. Just before the pitch, Burright had been moved toward the first-base side. "Who moved Burright?" Ron asked, as if he didn't know. It was Durocher, doing what he did a lot of—undermining Alston's authority. Durocher's reasoning was that Kuenn hit the ball to right field a lot.

Roebuck struggled with his control after that blown opportunity and walked the next two batters. The guys on the bench were going nuts. With Willie Mays now at the plate, Don Drysdale wanted to come in and put out the fire, but Alston told him to sit down, that he would be starting Game 1 of the World Series against the Yankees. Well shit, we've got to get there first.

Willie Mays singled off Roebuck's hand, and our lead was down to one run. Then Alston brought in Stan Williams, who had some control issues, too, instead of Drysdale. Oh man, the guys on the bench were just losing it at this point. And on the field, we just wanted to get out of it. A double-play ball. Something. But Orlando Cepeda hit a sacrifice fly to tie the game after Stan intentionally walked Ed Bailey to load the bases. Then Stan walked Jim Davenport to give the Giants the lead. Jose Pagan then hit a grounder that was bobbled, and another Giant run scored and they led, 6-4, just like that. Unbelievable. We couldn't muster anything in our half of the ninth, and just like that, the World Series, which had been in our grasp, was gone.

It was a madhouse in our clubhouse. There was still champagne and beer in there because we were supposed to be celebrating. We locked the doors and didn't let the press in. I was thinking, "If we win this thing, I could be MVP." It wasn't meant to be, though. I was young but I was outraged. I was just saying things, yelling things at Alston. Johnny Podres remembers me saying, "You took my Goddamn money." I was talking about bonus money, money for playing in the World Series. Alston was in his office with the door closed, but I was shouting it toward him anyway. "Goddamit, you took my Goddamn money." There was a table where we signed balls in the middle of the room and it was really heavy, stabilized. I didn't realize at the time just how heavy and stabilized it was . . . until I kicked it in anger. I just hopped around on one foot, still yelling. That hurt. But not as much as blowing that chance to beat the Giants and play the Yankees in the World Series. I was the last one out of the ballpark.

Alston almost paid for the collapse with his job. Word was that Mr. O'Malley wanted to fire him in favor of Durocher or Pete Reiser, but Buzzie Bavasi stuck up for his manager. Buzzie said that Alston wasn't the one who made the errors, and that if Alston went, he went too. O'Malley backed off. But some players were made out to be scapegoats. Stan Williams, who shouldn't even have been in the game in the first place—Drysdale should have been—was traded to the Yankees for Bill "Moose" Skowron. Burright, who was positioned wrongly, and Duke Snider, the Duke of Flatbush from the Brooklyn days who claimed responsibility for locking the clubhouse doors on the reporters, were also sent to New York, though they went to the awful Mets. And Roebuck was shipped off to the Washington Senators.

Bittersweet Winter

The 1962 season was the most bittersweet season I ever had. Sure, I had a great personal campaign at the plate, but we lost that playoff to our biggest rivals, the San Francisco Giants, and they got to go to the World Series while we got to go home for the winter. *The Sporting News* did a nice article and cartoon on me, though, and it took some of the sting away, but not all of it. There was still some salt in the wound. They called me "The Forgotten Man of the Dodgers"; the headline of the one-page spread in the December 22, 1962 issue read, "D Stands for Davis, Dodgers and Dynamite."

The article described me as follows: "A quiet, unassuming type, only now has he emerged from the shadows of the Dodgers' big names." And there I was, a cartoon, with shadows, which looked like ghosts of my teammates Sandy Koufax, Don Drysdale, Frank Howard and Maury Wills creeping up behind me. The article continued: "Tommy's hitting has been a symphony of consistency just as effective on the road as at home. He has one of the sweetest level swings in the game." It also pointed out that I was the first Dodger to lead the National League in three different offensive categories: batting average (.346), RBIs (153) and hits (230). My batting average was the highest for a Dodger since Dixie Walker hit .357 in 1944, three years before Jackie Robinson integrated the game.

Something I didn't know at the time, but thanks to *The Sporting News* I'll never forget, was that at the time, I was only the sixth player to collect at least 150 RBIs in a single season, after such Hall of Famers as Hack Wilson, Chuck Klein, Ducky Medwick,

Rogers Hornsby and Mel Ott. In fact, my RBI total broke the Dodger record of one of my heroes: Roy Campanella had 142 ribbies in 1953. I still hold the Dodger record and I'm proud of that.

But perhaps what I was most proud of that year was how I played against the Giants. As *The Sporting News* reported, "He was a true Giant killer. In 21 games against San Francisco in 1962, Tommy batted .452 with eight home runs and scored 21 runs in 84 at-bats." In the third and deciding playoff game against the Giants, I even hit a home run off Juan Marichal in the sixth inning to put us up, 3-2. Then they came back, unfortunately. I don't think I'll ever get over blowing the 1962 pennant. It still upsets me to this day.

A Bad Break

As the 1965 season got rolling, I was just starting to hit the ball a little bit, because I overdid it in 1964. I tried to go for three batting championships in a row, and I put too much pressure on myself. And not just on the field. In 1964 my first wife lost her mother and I lost my father and my high school basketball coach. They all died that same year. After all that, I told myself, I'm going to go out and win another batting title, like it would heal me or something. I'm going to get three in a row. I was wrong. I didn't do well. I hit .275 after batting .346 and .326 the two years before.

Now, in '65, I started hitting the ball a little better and then I broke my ankle. It was May 1, 1965, and we were playing the Giants in front of a crowd of 50,000 at Dodger Stadium. I was on first and Ron Fairly hit a ground ball to Orlando Cepeda at first base. I ran to second, thinking I'd break up a double play and slide under Jose Pagan. But the closer I got to Pagan, who was on the inside of the base, the more I realized he wasn't going to get the ball. Cepeda had just gone to first base. I didn't have to do what I did.

So when I saw he wasn't going to get the ball, I crossed over to go to the bag with my left foot but my right back spike caught in

The broken right ankle that I suffered while sliding into second base early in the 1965 season forever changed my career. But making friends with guys like my replacement, Lou Johnson, made coming to the ballpark easier that year. Courtesy of the Los Angeles Dodgers

this Georgia clay they had in the infield at the time. It stayed there and my foot just turned around. My foot followed me and twisted around. They called it a spiral fracture because it went up the bone. My foot was folded up under me.

I was in shock. The trainer, Wayne Anderson, came out there and put my foot back in place. I didn't even know it. Then after they carried me off the field on a stretcher, they put me in some sort of balloon-type splint. It started to feel kind of good and I said, "Okay, I guess it's not as bad as I thought." But Dr. Kerlan came in, took off the splint and felt the ankle. He said, "Damn, it feels like there's a whole bunch of walnuts in there." I just said, "Oh no." He said, "Take him to the hospital," and that was it.

The whole time I just thought of Monte Irvin. He's in the Hall of Fame, but his career ended after he had a bad break too, the same kind of break. I thought, I'm done.

The First Visitor

A couple of weeks after the injury, the first player to come and see me in the hospital was Moose Skowron, and he wasn't even on the Dodgers any more. He was with the Chicago White Sox and they were in town to play the California Angels. I'll never forget that.

I ended up coming back for one game that season. I played in the last game of the year and grounded out. Then the Dodgers sent me to the Arizona Instructional League, where I played as a pinch hitter.

Returning From Injury

When I came back in 1966, I wasn't quite at full strength. Lou Johnson had a good season the year before, helping us win the World Series and we became quick friends. We split some playing time in left field. I didn't get up to bat as much as I would have liked to because I was still hurting a little bit, but I hit .313. I wasn't where

I could run like I wanted to. Lou picked me up, though. He picked all of us up.

"Tommy could run well, and I don't know what Tommy could have accomplished in his career if he had not turned his ankle around," Ron Fairly told a reporter.

The Champs Get Swept

We were the defending World Series champions and the Baltimore Orioles did to us in 1966 what we had done to the New York Yankees three years earlier—they pulled out the brooms for a sweep. The difference was we didn't expect to get to the World Series in 1966 and we made it there.

When we beat Philadelphia just to get there, we used up all our energy. We were spent and when we got to the World Series those three young boys just whipped our ass. Dave McNally, Jim Palmer and Wally Bunker went through us like Grant went through Richmond. We had no clue.

The Orioles were a good team, though. Frank Robinson had won the Triple Crown in the American League, and in Game 1 both he and Brooks Robinson hit home runs and they knocked Don Drysdale out of the game before the third inning. Their reliever, Moe Drabowski, struck out 11 and only allowed one hit and the Orioles beat us, 5-2. We didn't realize that we wouldn't score another run the rest of the series.

It was after the opener that Jim Palmer said, "You can beat the Dodgers with a fastball." It sounded cocky, but he was right. Palmer was only 20 years old and he was going against Sandy Koufax. Sandy was making his third start in eight days. None of us knew at the time that it would be his last game.

Palmer wasn't nervous at all. He grew up in Los Angeles, in Beverly Hills, and just stuck it to us. This was also the game when Willie Davis set a record by making three errors in center field after he lost balls in the sun. The rest of the team made three other errors, and the Orioles won Game 2, 6-0. In his last game, Sandy went six innings and gave up four runs, but only one was earned. The last batter Sandy faced was Davey Johnson, who would become the Dodgers manager in 1999.

Then it was on to Baltimore for Games 3 and 4 for the inevitable. Wally Bunker shut us out, 1-0, and then McNally did the same, 1-0. With a grand total of two runs, we set a record for fewest runs scored in the series. We were held scoreless by the Orioles for the last 33 innings of the series. It was shocking. We got swept. But we were in the World Series. In eight years in Los Angeles, the Dodgers had gone to the Fall Classic four times. They would not make it back until 1974, and they wouldn't win another World Series until 1981.

That's the Willie I Remember

Everybody makes errors. It's just that when you make them on the biggest stage, where everyone can see you, they have more of a lasting impression. I think Willie Davis got the short end of the stick, because for every error he made, he made up for it with a spectacular play. That's what I remember about Willie and the 1966 World Series against the Baltimore Orioles.

They do not talk about that catch he made in the Series. All they talk about are his three errors in Game 2 at Dodger Stadium, when he lost balls in the sun and threw a ball away. But that catch in Game 4 was amazing. The Baltimore Orioles' power-hitting first baseman, Boog Powell, hit a long drive to center field in the fourth inning of Game 4 and Willie raced back to the fence at full sprint. He leaped high and extended his right hand way over the top of the fence where he caught the ball. His midsection was at the top of the fence.

That's the Willie Davis I remember, making spectacular plays. Not the one who made three errors in one game and was killed by reporters and fans for it.

Salt in the Wound

After we were swept by the Baltimore Orioles in the 1966 World Series, we went on a tour of Japan. The embarrassment was far from over. And the drama was just beginning. On the tour of the Land of the Rising Sun, we played 18 games as was common then. Most major league teams would go over there for the tour and would be expected to go 16-2, 17-1, 15-3, maybe 14-4—something respectable like that. Well, we went 9-8-1. And we had a hard time doing that.

They were kicking our ass! Alston was getting pissed, boy. We lost four times to the Tokyo Yomiuri Giants, who were led by Sadaharu Oh, Japan's all-time home run king with 868 homers. The Giants had won the Japanese version of the World Series. Even in Japan we had trouble with a team known as the Giants.

We were partying, man. We were out there. Willie Davis and I almost got killed. We were in a cab one night and we got in a wreck. The cab went under a truck. We were covered in glass from the windows. The top of the cab had been shaved off.

The tour of Japan was becoming a tradition for the major leagues. The Brooklyn Dodgers had gone in 1956, and word had it that it was at the beginning of the trip, when the Dodgers stopped off in L.A. on the way over, that Mr. O'Malley first met with city officials about the possibility of moving to Southern California. The Dodgers went back in 1993 while the San Francisco Giants toured in 1960 and the Detroit Tigers went in 1962. None of those teams lost more than four games.

We had a good excuse, though. A lot of our guys chose not to go to Japan, saying they were tired or injured or both. Sandy Koufax,

Don Drysdale, Don Sutton, Wes Parker and Jim Gilliam skipped the tour. And Maury Wills left halfway through. He was upset that he had to go in the first place after trying to beg off because his right knee had been bothering him the entire regular season. So midway through the tour, he took off on an unexcused leave. What made matters worse was that Maury had a layover in Hawaii. On the layover he made a pit stop, and a picture of Maury playing his banjo in a Honolulu nightclub found its way to the newspapers. Walter O'Malley was furious. He wired Buzzie Bavasi, who, by the way, was not on the tour either, and demanded that Maury be traded . . . immediately. He'd get his wish, but something else would go down first.

Sandy Retires

Two days after playing our final game in Japan, where we lost our last four games, Sandy Koufax shocked the world when he held a press conference at the Beverly Wilshire Hotel in Beverly Hills to announce his retirement. He didn't go to Japan, so we didn't know what was happening. It was out of the blue. He was only 30 years old. I couldn't believe it.

I thought he was too young to retire. But he had problems with his finger and his elbow. On November 18, 1966, Sandy told the reporters, "I don't regret one minute of the last 12 years, but I think I would regret one year that was too many." He was getting out on top. Remember, he won 27 games that year, despite all the painkillers he had to take because his arm hurt so much. He said that half the time he felt high out there on the mound.

"I was getting cortisone shots with pretty good regularity, and I just feel like I don't want to take a chance on completely disabling myself," he said. A reporter asked him about his financial situation and Sandy was quick to answer. "If there is a man who did not have use of one of his arms and you told him it would cost a lot of money and he could buy back that use, he'd give him every dime he had, I believe." Sandy also said later that he never missed a start. "I've got a lot of years to live after baseball and I just would like to live them with complete use of my body."

Not too many people knew it, but Sandy had been battling arm problems for a while. In 1962, he had what was called Reynaud's Phenomenon.

"That's where his index finger went ice cold because of some nerve damage and he couldn't feel the ball," Vin Scully remembered. "And Sandy's left elbow was starting to pull up to where his arm was bent at an angle. He couldn't extend his arm. We talked about him retiring and he said to me, 'Yeah, I could play another year or so, but if I keep playing, this arm is going to be up here and I won't be able to play golf. And I'd like to play golf until I'm 70 years old.' That was one of his big concerns."

I was worried about me, though. There had been a rumor that I was on the trading block.

Trade Bait

As the 1966 season drew to a close, I had been hearing these rumors that I was about to be traded. My mother still lived in Brooklyn and even she heard that I was coming to the Mets. So I went to Buzzie and I asked him if I should go to Japan with the team for the tour. He said, "Don't worry about it. Just go and have a good time." Well, there had been stories out there that the Dodgers thought I was babying my leg. Goddamnit, I was still hurt. Dr. Kerlan even said so.

It was Tuesday, November 29, 1966, and I was playing golf in L.A. with Willie Davis. A reporter came up to me on the course— he was waiting for me at the end of nine—and he asked about my reaction to being traded to the Mets. I said, "I don't know anything about it. You're the first person to tell me." He said, "Oh, you did-n't know? Oh, sorry." He was embarrassed.

My mother was happy, because as she saw it, I was coming home. I was pissed. My immediate family in L.A. didn't like it either, but what can you do, it's a business. They stayed here in L.A. Everybody was in school, what are they going to do?

Dr. Kerlan told the Dodgers to give me two years to recuperate because I had a real bad injury and it would take that long to get me back at full strength. They traded me after one year. So I was deter-mined to come back after they traded me. That's why I tell every-body that the best year I ever had was 1967 with the Mets. I hit .302 for a last-place club and that enabled me to play until 1976 because I hit the ball on a bad ankle. Forget all the statistics. That was sur-vival.

Maury's Gone

Nate Oliver was Maury's roommate for the tour of Japan. And Nate said he may have had a hand in Maury's decision to leave for home midway through the tour.

"I got Maury fired," Nate said with a laugh. "When we went to Japan, Maury felt that he was an integral part of the team. And since the Big Two of Sandy and Don didn't have to go, Maury felt that he too should not have had to go. Maury's knee had been bothering him all season. He said, 'Look at this,' and he pointed to his knee. Mind you, he still had his pants on and I could see that his knee was still swollen, even through his trousers.

"So he asked me, 'If you were me, what would you do?' I told him that I couldn't make that decision, but I would look out for my own career and my own well being. Well, the next morning I woke up and unbeknownst to me, Maury was gone. He left. It was so embarrassing for Mr. O'Malley because he had to go to the emper-or of Japan and publicly apologize for Maury leaving.

"So they dispatched him—I can't think of a better word than 'dispatched'—when they traded him to the Pittsburgh Pirates. I felt kind of bad." Not as bad as Maury did. He was in tears.

The Dodger Dynamic Changes

Sandy retired on November 18. I was traded 11 days later to the Mets along with Derrell Griffith for Ron Hunt and Jim Hickman. Maury was dealt on December 1 to the Pittsburgh Pirates for Bob Bailey and Gene Michael. In 14 days late in 1966, the dynamic of the Dodgers changed dramatically.

"We lost three very, very intricate parts," Nate Oliver told a reporter. "Our best pitcher, the RBI man and easily the best player."

The way I saw it, they had to get new guys in there to start the Garvey and Cey era of the 1970s.

11

NO LONGER
BLEEDING BLUE

You Know What I Want

It took a while to get over the Dodgers trading me, but I always felt like I was a Dodger at heart. That's the team that I grew up rooting for, and that's the team that helped me realize my dream of playing in the major leagues. So even after I left the team, I still had friends in that dugout. Close friends. So close that they helped me out while I was in a New York Mets uniform.

It was the next-to-last game of the 1967 season, my first season away from the Dodgers, and we were playing at Dodger Stadium. I was zero for two at the plate that day when I stepped into the batter's box for my last at-bat of the game. On the season, I was hitting either .299 or .300. I had two strikes on me.

So I stepped out of the box and began wasting time by picking up dirt. I looked at my good friend, Dodger catcher John Roseboro. I said, "Johnny," under my breath. He heard me because he said in that voice of his, "What?"

Johnny Roseboro (left) was a mentor of mine early in my career with the Dodgers. We talked a lot during spring training, and after I left the team we talked some more. From behind home plate he helped me bat over .300 during my first year away from the Dodgers. Courtesy of the Los Angeles Dodgers

I told him, "I'm hitting .300 or .299 right now. I don't want to hit .200-something."

He said, "Oh, I didn't know that. What do you want?"

"You know what I want," I said. "Just give it to me right where I can hit it."

I'll be damned if Don Drysdale didn't put it right there for me and I hit a double. I got to second base and I said, "Time out. Come get me." We were in last place anyhow. We had already lost 100 games. So, they took me out of the game and I ended up batting .302 that season.

Blackballed for Helping Blue

Later in my career, I was playing with the Oakland Athletics and living with two roommates in a triplex in the downtown ghetto in Oakland, the Acorn Projects. I became friends with Vida Blue and Mudcat Grant.

When Vida Blue first came up, he was so exciting to watch that he would bring 10,000 extra people to the ballpark on days that he was pitching. He became so popular that people wanted him to make appearances and endorse stuff, so I helped him out a little bit. He was making $500 or a $1,000 an appearance. Then they started paying him big money so I told him, "You need somebody to represent you. I have a lawyer friend who's helped me a little bit, and he's helped Jerry West of the Lakers in the NBA. His name is Bob Gerst."

I introduced him to Bob, and the rest of the season he got him three endorsements, on which he earned $77,000. After Vida won the Cy Young and MVP Award in 1971, Vida asked Bob Gerst to represent him as he negotiated his new contract with the A's.

Players just didn't do that with A's owner Charlie Finley. A player didn't negotiate with Finley. Finley would say, "I'll give you $30,000 and that's it." Vida wanted $102,000. Finley was pissed at Vida and Gerst.

That same year, I hit .324 with nine game-winning RBIs—the same as Reggie Jackson—and scored 26 runs in only 79 games. So that winter, Gene Mauch came up to me and said, "Why is Finley mad at you?" I didn't know why. I had just had a good year, and we were in the playoffs.

During spring training in 1972 I was hitting .500, nine for 18. But I noticed the manager, Dick Williams, started acting a little shitty towards me. We were in Yuma and Dick came up to me and said, "Tommy, I'm going to have to let you go."

I was like, "Get out of here. You're kidding me."

"No, no, no. I've got to release you, Tommy," he repeated.

"But I hit .324. Why the hell are you talking about releasing me?"

What happened was, Finley had to show strength. He wanted to know who introduced Vida to the lawyer and they found out that I introduced the two. He couldn't get rid of Vida so he got rid of me. And I didn't get a job until late that summer. Nobody would touch me until July, when the Chicago Cubs signed me.

Ain't It Ironic?

Ron Fairly's Dodger career came to an end on June 11, 1969, when he was traded to the Montreal Expos . . . for Maury Wills.

"That was ironic that it happened and it was the worst thing that happened to me," Ron said years later. "I went from the Dodger organization to Siberia, or the baseball equivalent. I went up to Montreal. When O'Malley got rid of me, he got me out of the country.

"It was hard going from the Dodgers, an organization that expected to go to the World Series every year, to an expansion team. That was completely foreign to me, not only playing in Montreal but playing up there in 30-degree weather all the time. That wasn't fun at all."

I had played in Montreal in the minor leagues and I had a good time there, but the stadium the Expos played in when they first started out had bad sightlines for the batters. The sun set in left field, right over the shortstop.

"If you hit a ground ball to the shortstop and he threw the ball, you couldn't see it," Ron said. "So we had to have about a 10-minute delay in the game until the sun went down. They'd start the games at that time at eight o'clock and the sun would sit right there and there was no way you could see much of anything because it was right on top of the shortstop."

An era came to an end at the close of the 2004 season when Major League Baseball announced that the Expos would be moving to Washington, D.C. I guess you could say the sun finally and truly set on major league baseball in Montreal.

Upper Deck or Lower Deck?

Roger Craig was a Dodger from the Brooklyn days who came to Los Angeles with the team in 1958. But when the New York Mets opened shop for the 1962 season, they chose Roger, a right-handed pitcher, in the expansion draft. He only played two years for the Mets, but he had the chance to play for one of the game's most endearing personalities in Casey Stengel. Stengel was managing the team at that time. He referred to the Mets as 'The Amazins.' They were Amazin', he said, because they were so amazingly bad in their early days.

Roger told Ron Fairly about a pregame pitcher's meeting Casey held prior to one of his starts.

"The Mets were playing the Giants at the Polo Grounds and at that time, Willie McCovey was hot. He was hitting balls all over the National League," Ron said. "Casey has the meeting and he says, 'Roger, we're going to go over the hitters now. This Jose Pagan, he's a pesky hitter who sprays the ball around. If you just keep the ball in on him and you change speeds a little bit, you can get him out.'

"Roger says, 'Yeah, OK.'

"Then Casey said, 'Now, Roger, this Willie Mays, don't worry about him, because nobody's figured out how to get him out yet so you just do the best you can. Now, this McCovey kid, where do you want your right fielder, in the upper deck or lower deck?'

"Everybody started laughing, and that was the end of the meeting. Casey didn't cover any more hitters."

If the Giants had been playing in its current waterfront stadium, SBC Park, back then, Casey would have asked Roger if he wanted his right fielder to get a canoe. The Giants honored Willie by referring to the body of water on the other side of the right field fence as McCovey Cove. After all, Willie is in the Hall of Fame and he led the National League in home runs three times in his 22-year career, hitting 44 homers in 1963, 36 homers in 1968 and 45 homers in 1969.

We're Going to Fight

When I was with the Oakland A's I had a little bit of a confrontation with the man who would go on to become Mr. October. Reggie Jackson was just coming into his own and we bumped heads in the clubhouse. He was always getting on guys, putting them down. He was very articulate and well educated, and he used that to put guys down.

So we were sitting at our lockers one day and I just said, "You know, you're a leader. Go out there and lead. You don't need to put these young kids down."

I came from a winner with the Dodgers and we didn't do that so I guess it was just a clash of philosophies.

Reggie just looked at me and said, "Before the year's up, we're going to fight."

I said, "What are we waiting for? Let's go outside right now."

And we were the best of friends afterward. I guess his philosophy worked, too, because the A's won three straight World Series—in 1972, 1973 and 1974. Of course, it was after I was gone from Oakland.

You Get What You Pay For

Al Ferrara was another former Brooklyn schoolboy star who had that bittersweet feeling of playing for the Dodgers after they left the borough. That old joke about the only way to get to Carnegie Hall is "practice, practice, practice" was especially true for Al. He was a trained pianist who played in concerts at Carnegie Hall as a youngster; but when he was 16 years old he decided to concentrate on baseball.

He was an all-around good player in the minor leagues, leading the Florida State League in fielding and the California League in hits and runs. He was eventually named to the Southern Association All-Star team. But it was after he left the Dodgers that he made a mark on Sparky Anderson, another former Dodger.

Al was selected by the San Diego Padres in the 1968 expansion draft. Three years later he was traded to the Cincinnati Reds, who were managed by Sparky, for an unheralded player named Angel Bravo. Ron Fairly said that in one of Al's first games in Cincinnati, he lost a fly ball in the sun and the runner advanced on his error. After the inning, Al, who was also known as "The Bull" because of his strength, made his way to the Reds' dugout, and Sparky was there waiting for him at the top of the steps, just staring at him.

Al diffused the situation by simply saying, "Well, what did you expect for Angel Bravo?" He was trying to tell Sparky that you get what you pay for.

The Dodgers got their money's worth when Al broke up a no-hitter by the Chicago Cubs' Dick Ellsworth with a pinch-hit, three-run homer in May of '65. That home run ended up beating the Cubs, 3-1.

I'd Rather Sell Alternators?

If Moose Skowron was disillusioned when the Yankees traded him after nine years to the Dodgers in the winter of 1962, imagine his feelings when the Dodgers gave up on him before the All-Star break in his only season in L.A.

"I was angry because the Dodgers committed me to the Washington Senators in June," Moose said. "I happened to overhear a conversation that I was going to be traded and I was quite perturbed. After the World Series, the Dodgers tried to get out of the trade. They told me to tell the Senators that I would rather retire and sell alternators than accept the deal. That way the Senators would back out and the Dodgers would keep me. But baseball was my life then, I couldn't even threaten to retire. I wasn't even 33 years old yet."

So an honest Moose was cut loose by the Dodgers on December 6, 1963 and sent to Washington. He would be back home in the American League—the junior circuit—where he felt more comfortable. In his lone season in the National League, Moose batted just .203, but in 13 American League campaigns, his batting average was a robust .286.

Time Marches On

Even though it felt like time stopped when I was traded from the Dodgers to the Mets, time marched on for the Dodgers and their fans. I was no longer a Dodger, but that did not mean I stopped paying attention to them.

The 1967 season was one of upheaval for the Dodgers with Sandy retired and me and Maury traded away. Buzzie Bavasi was actually quoted as saying that because the fans did not expect the Dodgers to compete that year, the team was free to experiment. He

Bill "Moose" Skowron was disillusioned after joining the Dodgers in a trade from his beloved New York Yankees, but he became downright angry when he found out the Dodgers were going to ship him to the Washington Senators in a mid-season deal. Courtesy of the Los Angeles Dodgers was right about one thing—they did not compete. In fact, they finished in eighth place with a record of 73-89. Only the Houston Astros and my new team, the Mets, were worse in the National League. It was a year in which Lou Johnson broke his leg and the fans protested the Dodgers' poor year as attendance dropped by almost a million.

About the only positive to come out of the 1968 season was Don Drysdale's scoreless streak. Don did not allow a run for 58 2/3 innings that year, a record that stood for 20 years. Another Dodger came along and broke it. Orel Hershiser went 59 innings in 1988 and Don was there to see it because he was working as a broadcaster for the team. As a team, the Dodgers finished in seventh place with a record of just 76-86, 21 games behind the St. Louis Cardinals.

The 1969 season was another expansion year. The San Diego Padres and Montreal Expos joined the National League and baseball was split into two divisions and they added a round of playoffs. With Buzzie running things in San Diego, Al Campanis, the same man who signed me in Brooklyn, became the Dodger General Manager. One of his first acts was to bring Maury Wills back into the Dodger family, although he had to trade Ron Fairly to the Expos to get him and Manny Mota, the pinch-hitter extraordinaire. Willie Crawford finally broke into the Dodger lineup after taking over a starting spot in the outfield. But a link to Brooklyn was broken in early August when Don Drysdale retired. The durable Big D had never missed a start in his career until May of the '69 season when his shoulder began bothering him. And even though the Dodgers finished out of the race that year in fourth place with a record of 85-77, eight games behind the Atlanta Braves, my good friend Willie Davis kept Dodger Stadium buzzing with a club-record 31-game hitting streak.

The 1960s were finished and so was the First Golden Age of the Dodgers in Los Angeles. But the era is not completely gone. It still lives on in the memories of those who lived them and in the hearts of the fans who witnessed the men who wore Dodger Blue.

12

A WALK ON THE LIGHTER SIDE

The Show Must Go On

At the conclusion of a season, a group of us used to get invited to perform in Las Vegas. Of course we accepted. So we were doing Joey Bishop's show at the Sands Hotel, and Willie and I danced in the show. We would perform sometimes in our Dodger uniforms, and that probably wasn't such a good idea because the lights are right on us so the audience could almost see right through our uniforms. One night I was wearing boxer shorts that were like prison shorts—they had bars on them. And the people in the audience were looking up and laughing and pointing at me. They could see the damn shorts.

We were there during the peak of the holiday season. I had a routine where I played my Horner melodica. You would blow into it like a horn but play a keyboard like a piano. It's maybe a foot long and I played "Stella by Starlight," which is a nice little standard jazz tune. All I could do was play the tune; I couldn't improvise. And I played that every night.

The first show came on at 12 midnight and the second show was at two o'clock in the morning. Well, I had a couple hot toddies, a couple of drinks in between shows. So we're getting ready to play, and I forgot the song. I started playing and then I lost it. But I stayed in the key and it sounded like I was hitting it right, as if I was playing jazz. Then I caught myself. My first wife, she looked up at me like, "He doesn't play like that at home." But I stayed with it. The show goes on, you know. The conductor even looked at me like, "What was that?"

Music, Maestro

We all liked to dabble in music, and we were pretty good, too. After one game in New York against the Mets, me, Maury and Willie Davis were singing in the shower. Ralph Kiner, the Hall of Famer, was the announcer for the Mets at the time. He was in the clubhouse doing interviews and he overheard us.

Now he knew some people who knew some people and that led to us getting invited to sing on the *Today Show* . . . at five a.m. They wanted us to sing "Bye Bye, Blackbird." Maury could play some banjo, so we accepted the invite. Willie and I, though, were scared to death when we thought about it some more. So we no-showed.

But Maury showed up, and he went solo. He was always a showman. He loved that shit.

St. Pat's With the O'Malleys

Another time we used to perform was on St. Patrick's Day during spring training. Mr. O'Malley always had a huge party at Dodgertown in Vero Beach to celebrate the day that St. Patrick supposedly drove the snakes out of Ireland. Mr. O'Malley, of course, was Irish, and this was his special get together for him and his friends.

Maury played the banjo and Nate Oliver could sing like a bird, "Way down the riverside, whoa, whoa, way down the riverside, whoa, whoa." Nate could have been one of the greats, too, but he was always spending time shifting between the minors and big leagues, and once he did make it, he hurt himself by banging his knee on the right-field wall while chasing down a fly ball.

Riding Lew

Playing head games with your opponent is as old as playing the game itself. Sometimes it's even more fun, as Lew Burdette found out.

Lew was traded by the Milwaukee Braves to the St. Louis Cardinals in the middle of the 1963 season. We were in the pennant race with the Cardinals and we had a one-game lead late in the season. So we had to win these three games in St. Louis. They had won 19 out of 20 games coming into that series against us.

We won the first game, 3-1, with Johnny Podres on the mound. We started yelling across the field to the other dugout, "Hey, Lew, 19 for 21!" Then we won the second on a Sandy Koufax four-hit shutout, 4-0, and we shouted again, "Lew, 19 for 22!" Then in the third game, the Cardinals took a 5-1 lead in the third inning and they had Bob Gibson on the mound. But we were able to pull out the three-game sweep in 13 innings. Rookie first baseman Dick Nen, father of Giants pitcher Robb Nen, hit a game-tying homer with one out in the ninth inning of the eventual 6-5 win. It was Dick's only hit in a Dodger uniform, and it was a big enough blast that we voted Dick a World Series share of $1,000.

It also allowed us to yell over to the Cardinal dugout, "Hey, Lew, you're still on 19." I don't think Lew thought that was so cute, our yelling at him like that, especially since the Cardinals only won two more games the rest of the season. We ended up beating them out by six games to win the National League pennant and sweep the New York Yankees in the World Series.

Pipe Down, Honey

Perhaps the greatest pitching duel I ever took part in went down on June 18, 1962. We were playing the St. Louis Cardinals and Bob Gibson, one of the most intimidating pitchers of all time, was on the mound for them. We had Sandy Koufax going for us. It was truly a pitchers' duel for the ages, one that had both pitchers throwing shutouts into the ninth inning. That's when I hit a solo home run to beat Gibson, 1-0. It was the last of the ninth, and I hit it into the bullpen for a walk-off shot.

To celebrate, my first wife, Shirley, and I went to this restaurant-bar called Memory Lane after the game and Gibby was there. So I walked in and I went to make the proper introductions, saying, "Bob, this is my wife, Shirley." Keep in mind that Bob and I were friends.

My wife says, "Oh, this is the guy you hit the home run off?" Oh my God.

I just said, "C'mon, let's go home, baby. I'm dead. You just killed me."

He just looked up and said, "Yes, I'm the one that he hit the home run off."

But when he said it, it was like daggers were coming out of his mouth.

I said, "Oh, I'm dead, I'm dead, I'm dead. You can't say things like that. You just can't say things like that."

So we left. And then two weeks later I beat him again. I thought for sure he'd hit me later, but he never did. I mean, it's a wonder he never threw at me. He didn't think I was a threat, or at least a home run threat. But I beat him twice. I talked to Curt Flood about it a while later and he said, "You know, he still doesn't know why he didn't hit you." Maybe it was because I wasn't really a home run threat. I just happened to get lucky against him. But Gibby mentioned me in his book so I feel pretty good about it.

Maury said that those home runs were the by-product of Bobby Bragan, our manager in Spokane, chewing me out.

"Bragen was all over Tommy in Spokane because he wouldn't pull the ball," Maury said. "Well, that paid off against Gibson when he pulled that ball for a home run into the bullpen. I guess it was learned behavior."

I guess so, too. And if so, I'm glad.

It's Not Candy

A big part of Lou Johnson's personality was his lighthearted nature and his ability to successfully deal with grief. Lou is missing the tip of his right ear. He lost it, he said, in a car accident in Oklahoma while playing in the minor leagues. He had some prosthetics made, four different ones to match his skin color, and he had to keep them in the refrigerator when he wasn't wearing them so they would keep their shape and stay fresh. But his kids at the time were so young that they didn't know any better. They thought Lou's "ears" were pieces of chocolate candy and pulled them out and chewed on them.

Lou just laughed.

Getting into the Groove

There's a lot of down time when it comes to baseball. You're at the stadium for a few hours before the game even starts. So before the game, during batting practice, they'd play some music in the stadium over the loudspeakers. Not the organ, but some regular Top 40-type music, something with a groove to it.

I'd be moving and grooving to it out in the outfield. And Jim Gilliam didn't think that was quite proper. He would come out to me and say, "Um, you know what? You can dance after the game. Right now, the way you play defense, you should be catching some fly balls instead of dancing."

He'd make me feel bad. But I'd shake it off. He was right, though. I was terrible in the outfield.

Who's the Celebrity Now?

Because baseball was such a draw in L.A. and because we were always competing for a pennant, Dodger Stadium became an "in" place. We didn't necessarily have to go to Hollywood or Las Vegas to see the stars. They came to our games. A Dodger game was the place to see and be seen.

It was nice. Because I was a Dodger, I went to Frank Sinatra's abode out in Palm Springs. I've been to Milton Berle's house. He was a huge Dodger fan. I heard that Uncle Milty wanted to buy an ownership stake in the Dodgers when they first moved from Brooklyn in 1958 but Mr. O'Malley did not want partners. I knew Dean Martin and Sammy Davis Jr. Sammy used to always say to me, "Hello, namesake."

I also knew Joe Louis, the former heavyweight boxing champion. When Leo Durocher was a coach with the Dodgers, he married the actress Laraine Day, who played a nurse in those Dr. Kildare movies. So we'd go over to their house for parties. You never knew who you'd see at their house. I mean, we used to go to movie stars' houses for parties. It just came with the territory.

Another Dodgers fan that I really liked was Nat King Cole, the singer. I was a fan of his music. Connie Stevens and Doris Day

The stars came out to Dodger Stadium for the Hollywood Stars game, an L.A. baseball tradition. Here, Jackie Gleason beats out a throw to first—just ask umpire Annette Funicello. Courtesy of the Los Angeles Dodgers

would be at the stadium, sitting behind the dugout. Everybody loved the Dodgers. All over the world they knew about "Dem Bums" and our fans' favorite saying, "Wait 'till next year."

The tradition of celebrities coming to baseball games started with the old Hollywood Stars and Los Angeles Angels of the Pacific Coach League. But celebrities coming to Dodger games began almost as soon as the Dodgers moved to Los Angeles. They came in droves to the Coliseum.

Then they had their own game, the Hollywood Stars Game, that they would play on the field before we would play a regular game. They still play that game to this day. Back then, actors like Bob Newhart, Buddy Hackett, Steve Allen and Don Rickles and Jackie Gleason and Danny Kaye played in the Hollywood Stars game.

I went to Buddy's house once and he had a one-million-dollar collection of guns. They were all encased—big ones, small ones. A million dollar's worth.

The funny thing was, while they were all Dodger fans, I was actually a fan of theirs.

Foreign Substance

Jim Maloney was a great right-handed hurler for Cincinnati. He was the Reds' star pitcher for a while in the early and mid-1960s. He threw hard. One time when I was batting he said, "Hey, Tommy," from the mound. I responded, "What?" As I was looking at him, he stuck his finger up his nose and pulled out a big green one. It was big enough for me to see it standing 60 feet, 6 inches away at home plate. And then he put it on the ball. He threw me a booger ball. I didn't swing at it. I backed out. He laughed and thought that was so funny.

Hitting the Links

We weren't supposed to play golf, but we were addicted to the game. So we just had to be careful not to get caught. We wouldn't take our golf shoes on the road because that would have been just asking to get caught. Instead, they used to sell plastic covers that had the metal spikes on the bottom so you could just put them over your regular shoes. I'd just take those on the road with me. And then we would find clubs and buy balls and then it was off to the golf course.

Skinny Willie

With me in leftfield and Big Frank Howard in right field, poor Willie Davis had a lot of ground to cover from his position in centerfield.

The way Stu Nahan tells it, "You'd look out there and you'd see Tommy positioned 10 feet from the left-field foul line and Frank Howard was 10 feet from the right-field foul line. Any ball hit between Tommy and Frank, you'd just hear, 'C'mon, Willie.' And by the third inning, Willie's on his knees, dead tired."

That's right. We would say, "C'mon, Willie, let's go, baby. That's your ball. You got it." All that running around that he had to do to cover ground for Frank and me is what kept Willie so skinny.

Of Numbers and Nicknames

Every team has nicknames. We had a system where our uniform number was included in the name. The way Ron Fairly tells it, however, he had the most unusual moniker.

"We called Willie Davis '3-Dog.' Maury was '30-Dog' and Tommy was '12-Dog,'" remembered Fairly. "I was the '6-mule.' I was more like a diesel engine. I couldn't go very fast but I just kept right on going."

And then some of the guys were called something that they obviously were not. John Roseboro, who didn't say much, was known as "Gabby" and Nate Oliver, who was a skinny guy, was called "Brute" by Sandy. Everyone else called Nate "Pee-Wee."

Warning Track Power

Ron Fairly wasn't the biggest of guys, but he had some pop in his bat and he was an excellent contact hitter. Throughout his Dodger career he was known as Mr. Clutch, or Mr. Consistency. He had a great World Series in 1965 against the Twins. He hit safely in all seven games and collected 11 hits, scored the most runs of the series by crossing home plate seven times and led everybody with six RBIs and a .379 batting average. He might have won the MVP were it not for Sandy Koufax.

But while Ron could hit the ball out of the park, it seemed like more often than not, he'd always hit them right to the edge, to the warning track. He'd come back and his walk to the dugout was like Dennis the Menace—we could tell that he was mad. He'd start yelling, "This Goddamned park! It's too big for me."

One time he was so frustrated that when he went to put his bat back in the slot against the wall in the dugout, he flung it in there really hard. The back of the slot was concrete so when he threw that thing in there, it bounced out and flew right by Alston's head. Alston just picked it up and said, "Uh, Ron, next time you do that, I'm going to kick your ass."

Talking about it years later, Ron said, "I decided then I didn't want to do that anymore."

After that, Ron just put the bat in the slot nice and easy, even if he had just flown out to the warning track.

Go to the Right

Frank Howard was a monster at the plate and I always thought he had one of the best-ever throwing arms in the game until he hurt his elbow running into a wall and slamming it into the concrete. He could throw the ball in at chest-high from right field once he wound up and cut it loose.

Ron Fairly tells a story of how Frank once made like a pro football player—"Wrong Way" Jim Marshall, the Minnesota Vikings' Hall of Famer who one time recovered a fumble and ran it into the wrong end zone.

"Frank was leading off of second base, and he had it in his mind that when the ball was hit that he was going to go to his right," Ron said. "I told him, 'That's good, Frank, you've got this figured out pretty good that when you're at second base and there's a base hit you go to your right.' There was a soft line drive hit into left field and Frank went halfway between second and third and turned completely around and looked into left field. When the ball landed he said to himself, 'I'm going to my right.' He went back to second base."

It's amazing we didn't call him "Wrong Way" Frank. He was too big to make fun of, anyway.

The Mooooooose Is Loose

You could always tell someone's personality by who they chose as their roommate on the road. Moose Skowron and Frank Howard were like two peas in a pod . . . two very big peas in a smallish pod. Ron Fairly, though, said there was a method to the Dodgers' madness in pairing the gargantuan twosome together.

"We roomed Moose with Frank Howard because we didn't want to screw up two rooms," Ron said. "When Moose would call you on the phone, he would say, 'Tell Ron that Mooooooose called.' He'd stretch it out, 'Mooooooose.' One day we had a rainout in Chicago, so we were looking for something to do in the early afternoon. We decided we were going to go to a movie. So Moose said, let me call my roommate and see if he wants to go.

"Moose was on the lobby phone and he called up to the room: 'Hello, Frank, Mooooooose.'

"And Frank said, 'I'm sorry, but he's not here,' and then he hung up on him."

Popcorn? What Popcorn?

Frank Howard may have crushed the ball at the plate and had a fantastic throwing arm, but he was always good for a laugh, even if it was at his expense.

"We were playing at Wrigley Field one day and it's a close ball game and there's a ball hit into right field and Frank goes back next to the ivy," Ron remembered. "Frank kind of leaps in the air and some fan out there has a great big bucket of popcorn and he poured it right on top of him. And Frank missed the ball, runners scored and Alston ran out of the dugout.

"Augie Donatelli was the umpire and Alston ran out and said, 'Fan interference! The popcorn came down and bothered Frank and he couldn't make the catch.' It looked like Alston was going to win the argument. Until Augie Donatelli went out and he says, 'Frank, did the popcorn bother you?' And Frank said, 'What popcorn?' And with that, Alston turned around and walked off the field. That was it. He couldn't say anymore."

But we said a lot to Frank in the dugout.

Play (Well) or Pay

Every time we played in Chicago we had a lot of free time. And many opportunities to create a funny story or two. Ron Fairly remembers this one time we were in Chicago for a crucial four-game series with the Cubs.

"The first night we got in there early and Buzzie Bavasi was coming back at about 11 o'clock at night down Michigan Avenue and there was a cocktail lounge and he saw a couple of our pitchers sitting in the bar having a drink," Ron said. "So he kind of got upset over that and he thought, 'I don't have to check their rooms because I know they're not going to be in by midnight,' which was curfew.

"So he went to somebody else's room to check and they weren't in and he didn't want to get more irritated so he decided, 'I'm not going to check anymore because the more guys I check, the more aggravated I'm going to be.'

"So the next day, we're taking batting practice and getting ready for the series and we're called back off the field to have a meeting. We had a rule on our ballclub that if you were out after curfew it cost you $100. So in his meeting, Buzzie bluffed and said, 'You know, last night I checked everybody's room,' and he pulled out an envelope from his coat and continued, 'I have a list of all the rooms that I checked last night. And if your name is on this list and you don't come into the trainer's room'—and the trainer's room wasn't that large—'it's going to cost you $500.'

"So you're sitting there saying to yourself, 'Do I want to be fined $100 or $500?' And Buzzie says it again, 'I have everybody's name here. All the guys that were out late last night, you want to go up to the trainer's room.' We couldn't get everybody in the room.

"So we went back out to the clubhouse and Buzzie said, 'Okay, here's the deal, if you don't win three out of four, I'm going to get everybody for 100 bucks.' And Johnny Podres pitched the last game and we won, taking three of four from the Cubs. Johnny says, 'I can really win those pressure games.' He saved everybody $100."

That's what you call a big-money pitcher.

Buzzie the Prankster

A lot of the guys loved heading to the track whenever they had free time. Betting on the ponies was almost as big a pastime as baseball. Buzzie Bavasi once saw Johnny Podres, Don Zimmer and Al Ferrara at the track the day of a game and played a trick on the three of them when they arrived at the ballpark. He waited until they were back and already in uniform before he put notes in their lockers that said, "Before you put your uniform on, come up and see me." But Buzzie was just having some fun with them, acting like he was all upset.

All three of them went up to Buzzie's office and they were a little bit nervous. They didn't know what the hell was going on.

"Buzzie asked them, 'Where were you guys today?'," remembered Ron. "They said, 'We didn't do anything.' So, Buzzie asks, 'Were you at the track?' Their faces got real funny and they said, 'Yeah, we were at the track.' So then Buzzie said, 'Okay, then why were you late getting to the ballpark?' But Buzzie timed it so that they wouldn't get the message until after they had their uniforms on. Podres says, 'We had a flat tire.'

"So Buzzie took out a piece of paper and tore off some pieces and handed them each a pencil and said, 'Okay, write down which tire was flat.' Buzzie looked up and they had all written down a different tire. Buzzie just laughed and told them to get out of there."

Buzzie liked pulling jokes on people. Especially when it came to negotiating contracts with players. But the jokes were always on the players. Back before free agency and the influx of agents, players had to represent themselves when they went into contract talks with the club. Buzzie did not like it when a player went in asking for more money, even if he deserved it. He told me once he would pay me anything I wanted, just so long as I had the exact same season as the year before. Well, I couldn't guarantee that, of course.

On a related note, Ron experienced a true Buzzie moment.

"I was looking at getting a pretty good raise," Ron said. "So I went in to negotiate and they had just made the announcement that Tommy Davis and Frank Howard had signed. Somewhere during the course of my conversation with Bavasi, he said, 'We just signed Tommy and Frank and here's the contracts.' Edna, his secretary, rang him at that moment and said he was needed out front. So he gets up and leaves the office and leaves those 'contracts' on his desk for me to see. They weren't worth very much and I'm thinking, 'They had great years and I had a good year.' So I thought, 'Hell, maybe I'm not worth as much as I think I am.' Buzzie cheated me for about $10,000."

Buzzie did that kind of stuff all the time. He did it to me by leaving Maury's fake contract out there for me. But one time Johnny Podres got Buzzie back. Johnny told Buzzie to go ahead and fill out the contract, that he agreed to any terms. Buzzie was uncomfortable with that because it took the power of negotiation away from him. It made Buzzie wonder if he overpaid. Johnny got Buzzie another time as well when Johnny owed Buzzie $500 as a fine. He called Buzzie from the track and asked if he wanted to double his money. He said he had a tip on a real long shot and Buzzie said to go ahead and make the bet. But after Buzzie hung up, the light went on over his head and he turned and looked at his assistant and said, "I just lost $500." The assistant said, "What do you mean? The race hasn't even happened yet." So Buzzie said, "Yeah, but Johnny didn't tell me the name of the horse."

A Free Spirit

Mike Kekich was a left-handed relief pitcher who would water ski on his off-days. He was called "another Sandy Koufax" when he was signed by the Dodgers in 1964. A year later, in the summer of 1965, he was married. He and his bride honeymooned in Santa Barbara. Sounds nice, right? Until you realize that they were both injured in a motorcycle accident.

Mike also accomplished the equivalent of getting fired on your day off—he was thrown out of a game by the umpires before he even got into the game. That took some talent. The umps apparently did not like the way he was riding them and talking trash from the bench.

But he was perhaps best known for the trade he pulled off when he was with the Yankees in 1973. Kekich and Fritz Peterson, a teammate with the Yankees, traded wives, children and houses. And this was before the advent of reality television. He was just about 30 years too early.

Last One Out, Turn Off the Lights

After we clinched the pennant and our spot in the 1965 World Series against the Minnesota Twins, we got smashed. The champagne and beer were flowing. We were celebrating in the clubhouse, spraying everybody with champagne. By the time our clubhouse celebration was over, it was totally dark outside and we left to go home to change and come back to celebrate that night in the Stadium Club with everyone else in the organization.

Jim Brewer, who had come to the Dodgers in a trade with the Cubs the year before, was so smashed that he never went home. He was in the trainer's room sleeping and the place was totally dark. There was nobody in the whole damn stadium and he was asleep in the trainer's room. In the dark. Somebody went and got him some clothes and woke him up to join the official celebration. It was great.

Atomic Balm, Anyone?

Sandy needed all kinds of help to get him over the pain in his pitching arm. He used to lather up with this hot lotion called Atomic Balm and put on a sweater to trap the heat and keep his arm loose. We were playing in Pittsburgh one night and Lou Johnson was cold so he decided to wear Sandy's sweater to stay warm. He didn't keep it on for long. The stuff burned him and he tore off that sweater quick.

"It was too warm for me," Lou said. "I had to take off the sweater and get some rubbing alcohol and rub that stuff off in the trainer's room."

He also gained an appreciation for Sandy's pain tolerance. "With as warm as that stuff was," Lou said, "after that I felt I did know the strength of the man."

Thanks for the Memories

We were the toast of the town after sweeping the Yankees in the 1963 World Series. It seemed like everyone wanted a piece of us. It was an exciting time. Within a month of the final out of the series, Bob Hope had Sandy Koufax, Don Drysdale and myself as the "special attraction" for his *Chrysler Comedy Special* on television. It was a pretty big deal, some of the other guests were Andy Griffith, Martha Raye and Jane Russell. When Bob introduced us for our 12-minute sketch—that's a real long time on television—we came walking down this big staircase at the back of the stage. We were in total lockstep with each other and we were wearing tuxedos with tails and top hats and we had canes. Real classy. Bob started in on us right away and they gave Sandy all the best lines. He was Koufax, after all. I was just happy to be there.

"Yes, sir, this is what Casey Stengel dreams about," Bob said. "Hey, tell me Sandy, how does it feel to be a hero?"

"I don't know, we haven't finished this act yet."

After the crowd stopped laughing, Bob turned to me.

"You nervous, Tommy?"

"This is worse than playing third base," I said. "Don't throw anything my way until I get adjusted to these lights."

Sandy had the next line. "Don't be scared, Tommy, just think about the money we're getting here."

"That's what's making me nervous," I said.

I think I had good timing. That's when Don got in the act.

"Hey, Bob, if we blow a couple of jokes out here, what's the loser's share?" he asked.

"Look, I'm not going to worry about you, Don," Bob replied. "I've always had the utmost confidence in you."

"Well then, what's Koufax doing here? I've been out here two minutes, and already you've gone to the bullpen."

"Relax," Bob said. "Perranoski hasn't even got his makeup on yet. Now listen, I just want you guys to relax. Because if you make a mistake, we just stop and do it over."

Sandy had another classic one-liner: "I wish I could do that with the pitch I threw Mantle."

Bob did his homework when it came to us and the World Series, which had a record pool of $1,017,546.43.

"You guys divvied up the biggest World Series purse in history," he said. "Tell me, what are you going to do with all that loot?"

"Well," Don said with a shrug. "I'm married."

"I'm married too," I said. But before Bob could even ask Sandy, he piped in, "I'm going out and have a ball."

The crowd erupted as Bob congratulated Sandy, saying, "That's my boy, yes, sir."

Sandy then said, "You single, too?"

"No," Bob said, "I'm just reminiscing. Sandy, you struck out 15 batters for a World Series record. What's your secret?"

"There's no secret, Bob. I just do what you do," Sandy claimed.

"What's that?" Bob asked.

"I just wind up and throw it."

"Strange, it didn't come out that way in rehearsal," Bob said, before turning his attention back toward me.

"But getting back to you, Tommy, what happened to you playing third base? Did you make an error there?"

"Are you kidding?" I said. "I fumbled enough to play for the Rams."

The funny thing was, they had to work with me in rehearsal on my speech and on what syllables I stressed. I guess I still had too strong of a New York accent. Bob then showed some of our bloop-

They called us "The Big 4"—Don Drysdale, me, Sandy Koufax and Maury Wills. I'm just glad we performed better as a unit on the field than we did on the Bob Hope comedy special—without Maury, who was probably playing his banjo in Las Vegas anyway. Courtesy of the Los Angeles Dodgers

ers from the World Series. He showed the umpire having a conversation with Don, and Bob took it from there.

"Don, did you really use a spitball?"

Don acted like he was angry and he stepped up to Bob, who came up to about the middle of Don's chest.

"Do I look like a guy who would throw a spitball?" Don asked before Bob swallowed hard and said, "You look like two guys who would throw a spitball."

Bob showed some more bloopers, one of our outfielders having trouble.

"How about that, that's Davis, dropping the ball," Bob said as he stood next to me.

"Wait a minute," I said in protest, sticking to the script. "That's not me. That's Willie Davis. I'm the other Davis."

"Yeah, that's right," Bob said as he rocked on his feet. "Willie's the guy that won the batting championship."

"Nah, that's this Davis." I sounded like a little boy as I tapped my chest with my cane.

It was time for another classic exchange between Bob and Sandy as Bob asked him, "Sandy, you got Mickey Mantle out five times."

"Yeah, that's right."

"Then the sixth time, he hit a homer."

"That's right."

"Well, what happened there?"

"Mickey just hit the ball, that's all."

"What I mean is, how was that pitch different from the others?"

"It went further," Sandy replied.

Bob showed a mistake we made on the basepaths when two guys ended up on the same base.

"Boy, third base looked like a bus station," Bob said. "How'd that happen, Don?"

Don was quick with his reply, saying, "Well, that's a little strategy, Bob. We stole that play from the Mets."

It was hard to tell who had more fun that night, us, Bob or the audience. Especially when he showed us celebrating the win and everyone rushing Sandy on the mound after the final out.

"That's not affection, Bob," Sandy said. "I had the bottle opener in my pocket."

We needed it in the clubhouse celebration, where it rained champagne showers.

"Man, what a party," I said. "I hope I was there."

Don said the party looked like "an unemployment office in Texas" and Sandy said, "Looks like an AA meeting at Dean Martin's house."

Bob said the Yankees were under the sink drinking yogurt and then he set me up again. "Hey, Tommy, I didn't see you in that shot. Did you get any champagne?"

"I got so much, my sweatshirt is still hiccupping."

Our appearance on national television ended with a little song and dance—well, very little song and dance. That was my stuff, dancing. We did a take on "We're in the Money" and we sang, "We're in the money. The skies are sunny. We'll fire Alston, get us Doris Day instead. We never have to dally, with O'Malley, again. He wouldn't dare to threaten, that he'll trade us vets to the Colts or Mets. We're in the money."

Right after the show, Bob had one of his assistants come to me and say, "Mr. Hope would like to have dinner with you and your wife." So we went to his house in Toluca Lake and he had three par-3 holes in his backyard. He loved the game of golf. So do I. It was at night and the course was lit up with lights but I didn't get a chance to play. I wanted to, though.

Bob's famous song was "Thanks for the Memories." I couldn't have said it better myself. Not just for that evening of hanging out with Bob Hope, but for the time I spent living my dream and playing baseball for my hometown team. Even if I had to leave Brooklyn to do it.

Celebrate the Heroes of Baseball
in These Other 2005 Releases from Sports Publishing!

Brooklyn Remembered
by Maury Allen

- 6 x 9 hardcover
- 250+ pages
- photo insert
- $24.95
- 2005 release!

Cardinals:
Where Have You Gone?
by Rob Rains

- 6 x 9 hardcover
- 200 pages
- photos throughout
- $19.95
- 2005 release!

How About That!
The Life of Mel Allen
by Stephen Borelli

- 6 x 9 hardcover
- 250 pages
- photo insert
- $24.95
- 2005 release!

Albert the Great:
The Albert Pujols Story
by Rob Rains

- 8.5 x 11 hardcover
- 128 pages
- color photos throughout
- $19.95
- 2005 release!

Fred Claire: My 30
Years in Dodger Blue
by Fred Claire
with Steve Springer

- 6 x 9 hardcover
- 208 pages
- photos throughout
- $24.95
- 2004 release!

Bleeding Pinstripes: A Season
with the Bleacher Creatures
of Yankee Stadium
by Filip Bondy

- 6 x 9 hardcover
- 250 pages
- 25-30 photos throughout
- $24.95
- 2005 release!

The Dodgers Encyclopedia:
2nd Edition
by William F. McNeil

- 8.5 x 11 hardcover
- 472 pages
- photos throughout
- $39.95
- 2003 release!

Jerome Holtman On
Baseball: A History of
Baseball Scribes
by Jerome Holtzman

- 6 x 9 hardcover
- 250 pages
- photo insert
- $24.95
- 2005 release!

Carl Erskine's Tales from
the Dodger Dugout:
Extra Innings
by Carle Erskine

- 5.5 x 8.25 hardcover
- 219 pages
- photos throughout
- $19.95
- 2004 release!

Red Sox vs. Yankees:
The Great Rivalry
by Harvey and
Frederic Frommer

- 8.5 x 11 trade paper
- 256 pages
- color photos throughout
- $14.95
- 2005 Release!

All books are available in bookstores everywhere!
Order 24-hours-a-day by calling toll-free **1-877-424-BOOK (2665).**
Also order online at **www.SportsPublishingLLC.com.**